S0-AGK-233

insights on productivity

Ideas from Industry Professionals on Getting More Done in the Workplace

network for productivity excellence

network for productivity excellence

The Network for Productivity Excellence is a national network of independent business owners and corporate executives. The Network is dedicated to researching, developing and sharing practical ideas related to improving the focus, organization and productivity of employees in companies of all sizes.

This publication is designed to provide reliable information regarding the subject matter covered. It is sold with the understanding that the authors and publisher are not engaged in rendering psychological, legal, financial, or other professional advice. If expert assistance is required, the services of a professional should be sought.

Copyright © 2007 by the Network for Productivity Excellence

Published by Dawson Publishing
3410 S. Tournament Drive
Memphis, TN 38125

All rights reserved. This book may not be reproduced in whole or in part without written permission from the publisher except by a reviewer who wishes to quote brief passages in connection with a review written for inclusion in a magazine or newspaper. Proper credit required.

The *GO System*® and *Network for Productivity Excellence*® are registered trademarks of DME Training and Consulting.

Cover design: Venue Advertising

Printing in the United States

ISBN: 978-0-9758680-2-7

Authors of *Insights on Productivity*

Kathleen Alessandro

Barbara Browning

Nicole Chamblin

Chris Crouch

Sue DeRoos

Pat DeSanto

Barb Friedman

Janice Gentles-Jones

Kimberly Guay

Nancy Hagan

Ann Michael Henry

Christine Kominiak

Kay Kotan

Mary Kutheis

Julie Mahan

Sue McGeer

Beverly Miller

Carla Miller

Nicole Pittaluga

Stephanie Pyle

Cheryl Robertson

Patti Schliep

Keith Sterne

Jan Wencel

Insights on Productivity
Contents

Kathleen Alessandro
Energized Solutions, LLC
Dearborn, Michigan

313.381.9222
kna@energized-solutions.com
www.energized-solutions.com

Kathleen serves as president of Energized Solutions, LLC, a firm specializing in teaching organizations innovative ways to do more with less in the 21st century.

Kathleen has been a speaker at numerous national events and served as a consultant on two documentaries focusing on the permanent workforce changes: *Layoff*, and the NBC White Paper, *America Works When America Works*. She is currently president of the National Association of Women Business Owners (NAWBO) – Greater Detroit Chapter.

For over 30 years, Kathleen has helped organizations develop and maintain creative and competent employees. Clients value her straightforward and practical approach to problem solving. She utilizes humor and real-life experiences to drive her message home. When all else fails, she believes that all of life challenges can be explained, and in all likelihood resolved, through the lyrics of classic Motown music.

1
Hey – Got a Minute?
Kathleen Alessandro

What?

In a classic scene from the movie *The Sunshine Boys*, two vaudevillian comedians, Al Lewis (George Burns) and Willie Clark (Walter Matthau), share a mutual disdain for each other. Al jabs his index finger into Willie's shoulder...repeatedly poking him to make sure Willie is paying close attention. As he pokes Willie, Al continues to offer a never-ending flow of useful information. Finally, an exasperated Willie bellows... *"Again mit the finger...stop it mit the finger already!"*

Today's workplace is replete with a variety of "fingers" constantly jabbing our physical and virtual shoulders via e-mails, phone text messages, cell phone calls, instant messages, work phone calls and intrusive conversations with bosses, colleagues, etc. These interruptions are incessant, imposing and often inane.

The impact of workplace interruptions has become so significant that interruptions are the focus of academic studies in the fields of engineering, business management, computer science, etc. A cursory review of academic literature on the topic highlights such issues as "formal modeling of task interruptions," "context-aware computing to reduce the perceived burden of interruptions from mobile devices," and "factors defining face-to-face interruptions in the office environment."

For academically minded readers, you can begin to attack this problem by *allocating a significant portion of your temporal resources during each circadian period to focused and sustained cognitive activities free of co-species intrusions.* For those of you outside the loop of the lofty-minded academic world...*stop letting yahoos interrupt you all the time.*

Recent formal and anecdotal studies indicate that workplace interruptions range from once every three minutes to six times an hour. More significant is the fact that studies also indicate it usually takes a minimum of five minutes to return to productive work. Let's do the math. Assume six interruptions an hour and five minutes to return to productive work. Wait a minute; this doesn't even require breaking out the calculator. Can it be that workplace interruptions are chipping away 30 minutes of every hour...half of the workday? Shouldn't this be a breaking news story on CNN or the front page of *The Wall Street Journal?*

While my conversations with colleagues and clients seem to affirm this dilemma, check it out yourself. Keep records for a couple of days. Record how many times you are interrupted and calculate the average amount of time that it takes you to get back on track.

So What?

Whether you work for yourself in a home office, in a small business, in a major corporation or for a nonprofit, you probably get up and go to the "office" daily to conduct activities, create opportunities and take care of important issues. However, during a typical workday, interruptions significantly impact our workflow. Many of the more popular "time-saving" productivity gadgets and electronic communication devices help people create offices that are the equivalent of a 24-hour breaking news center. I'm expecting Wolf Blitzer to show up in many of my clients' offices any day now. E-mails ping, work phones ring, cell phone ringtones play songs, and instant-message services encourage people to share every thought and occurrence, creating a cacophony of sights and sounds that challenge everyone's productivity.

This bombardment of interruptions makes deep thinking and critical analysis almost impossible. Interruptions, even if they are worthwhile, always require you to reset your thought and work processes...where did you leave off, what were you thinking and doing before you were interrupted?

Now What?

So how can you restore order to your workday? Keep in mind that the workplace is a social enterprise where interaction and communication is important. However, it is more important to create an atmosphere where creative, focused and productive communication and activity is nurtured, while extraneous, redundant and inappropriate exchanges and interruptions are limited. Here are a few practical options to consider:

The 15 Square Inch Solution

Instead of sending numerous e-mails, making telephone calls and conducting walk-by conversations, use a 15 square inch solution to make your communications more thoughtful, powerful and focused. Consider using 3 x 5 "capture cards." Old-fashioned index cards might be the lowest tech, highest impact information storage and retrieval resource ever invented. Keep capture cards at your desk, in your pocket or purse, and available at all times. When an idea comes to mind regarding information you want to remember or share with a colleague, write it on a capture card and put the colleague's name or some sort of memory trigger on the top. As you complete these cards throughout the day, two things will occur:

1. You will capture quick passing thoughts, ideas, questions, tasks, etc., in a more organized and focused fashion.

2. You will be able to group these cards into related categories. As you prepare subsequent e-mails, memos, meeting agendas and project updates, your comments will be more detailed, coherent, organized and effective.

Set Up Hanging File Folders for Key People and Projects

Keep separate hanging files handy for your boss, your direct reports and a few other key people or projects. Drop the capture cards and other related notes and materials into the appropriate folders. Instead of frequently interrupting your colleagues or boss throughout the day, share a cup of coffee and a 15- to 20-minute focused conversation with appropriate information at hand. Ask your co-workers to do the same.

E-mail

Turn off the e-mail audio notification system. That "ping" will divert your attention each time you receive an incoming e-mail. Studies have shown that the majority of your incoming e-mails are of little or no value. Check your e-mail only between projects or tasks. Even better, set reasonable guidelines and times for checking your e-mail throughout the day, and otherwise ignore them. If possible, route electronic newsletters directly to a "Casual Reading" folder and review them at your convenience. Create a file for your supervisor and route all e-mails from it to a folder that you can review periodically. Reduce or eliminate all inappropriate e-mails. If people want to send, and you want to receive, humorous, inspirational or other inappropriate workplace e-mails, give them your home or personal e-mail address.

Set Up Your Office for Maximum Focused Productivity

Over the past few decades, workplace design has morphed from closed-door, individual offices to cubicles and wide-open employee pods. Regardless of your office setup, there are a few options worth considering. When you need a block of time for deep thinking, reading, processing and evaluating information, post a "Do Not Disturb" sign where potential visitors can easily see it. If possible, place your desk at a 90-degree angle to the entrance to minimize unnecessary interruptions as people pass by. Avoid putting "bait" in your workspace such as candy or gadgets that might attract people as they pass by.

Miscellaneous Interactions in the Workplace

People who love to go from office to office sharing personal, nonwork-related issues, gossip, anecdotes, etc., cause many interruptions. It is unreasonable to think that you can eliminate all these disruptions. It's just a normal part of any work environment. Have people put up notices of fund-raisers, get well card signings, congratulatory notes, office social events, etc., in a common area such as a break room or meeting room.

Consider putting an open forum whiteboard or bulletin board in the break room for comments and feedback regarding sporting events, office accomplishments and other office news. Occasionally schedule a few minutes at the end of staff meetings for personal or community updates. If you don't already have one, consider publishing a simple employee newsletter to deal with a lot of these more informal employee issues.

Manners and Office Protocol

Although we live in an era where casual standards rule, it is still important to establish certain office guidelines that promote mutual respect among co-workers. When walking through the office, assume that people are engaged in work and hold casual conversations to a minimum. Avoid hovering at someone's office door hoping they will look up from what they are doing and engage in a conversation with you. If they don't acknowledge your presence quickly, move on. Assume that it is only appropriate to share personal information with close friends and at appropriate times. Unless your visitor is the company psychiatrist or psychologist, assume that the correct answer to *"How are you doing?"* is *"Fine, thank you how are you?"* Not, *"My dog is sick."* or *"My spouse doesn't understand me."* or *"I ate something that is really doing a dance in my belly."* or *"My childhood was traumatic."*…and so forth and so on. Most people are already plagued with information overload and don't really care to hear about your personal problems. They were just trying to be sociable.

In summary, I'm not suggesting that you cut yourself off from any nonwork-related interactions with your co-workers. The key is finding the right balance. Interruptions are going to occur in the normal course of a typical day. Remember, you teach what you allow...so make sure you are not somehow inviting interruptions. And, don't assume they will just disappear on their own. Try some of the ideas I have shared with you or develop your own. Find ways to minimize the excessive "got a minute" office interruptions and maximize the enjoyment of having a highly productive day.

Barbara Browning
Order Within
Bayside, California

707.845.3611
Barbara@orderwithin.com
www.orderwithin.com

Barbara is a woman with a passion and mission to help people be better organized and more focused. Why? So they can be more productive, experience less stress and enjoy greater work/life balance.

Prior to establishing her organizing business, Barbara worked as an operations manager in the nonprofit sector and as a massage therapist for 20 years. Combining her operational and organizing skills with her commitment to well-being, she provides systems and solutions that help her clients reach their goals and achieve their missions.

Barbara lives, works and plays on California's north coast.

2
E-mail...Friend or Foe?
Barbara Browning

What?

If a person commits a crime by killing another person in a car accident, no one would think of arresting the car or charging the car with a crime. The car, in this situation, is the *instrumental cause* of death, not to be confused with the real cause. Maybe the *real cause* was speeding, reckless driving, driving under the influence of alcohol. Who knows? Maybe it wasn't a crime at all. Maybe it was an unavoidable accident. In all likelihood, law enforcement officials would be more interested in the *behavior* of the person driving the car, than the car. An inanimate object, such as a car, wouldn't be held responsible for the problem.

OK, I understand it is a bit of a leap in imagination to apply this situation to problems with e-mail. Or is it? If too many e-mails are *killing your productivity*, are you going to gain anything by blaming the e-mails? Are e-mails the real cause or simply the instrumental cause of the problem? Shouldn't you be more interested in the *behavior* of the person struggling with the e-mails?

In your situation, is e-mail a friend or foe? If e-mail appears to be your foe, are the incoming e-mails the real enemy? I think Walt Kelly, creator of the *Pogo* comic strip, said it best with his famous quote, "We have met the enemy and he is us." If you are struggling with e-mail, your behavior, or more specifically, your e-mail processing habits are likely the enemy. If your current habits are causing problems, you can only hope to solve the problems by changing your habits. As the saying goes, in the end, our habits become either the best of servants...or the worst of masters.

So What?

Human beings are supposed to be the most evolved creatures on Earth. The frontal region of the human brain is the most sophisticated resource available on the planet for dealing with life-enhancing functions such as planning, organizing, controlling impulsive behavior, assessing future consequences of current activities, and other issues referred to as the executive functions of the brain. People often compare the brain to a computer, however, the most powerful computers in the world still have nowhere near the comprehensive processing power of the roughly 3-pound, grapefruit-sized mass of tissue we call the brain. Why is this incredibly powerful mental resource being so easily overwhelmed by such a seemingly innocuous digital opponent as e-mail? Perhaps your priorities are unclear and e-mail is something easy to tackle. Perhaps you are using e-mail as an avoidance strategy. Who knows why the e-mails win out over more important priorities? While you are pondering the psychological or philosophical reasons that you pay more attention to e-mails than more important issues, let's get practical and map out a plan to solve this problem.

Now What?

There are some excellent books and articles on how to effectively manage e-mails and I often share tips from these resources with my clients. For example, a short and easy-to-read book titled *The Hamster Revolution* by Mike Song, Vicki Halsey and Tim Burress, offers a wealth of practical ideas on managing e-mail. Mark Hurst also wrote an interesting book titled *Bit Literacy* on strategies for managing the flow of digital information from various electronic sources, including e-mail. The resources addressing this problem are almost endless. A Google search on "e-mail tips" provides 465,000,000 results. However, I'm not sure sorting through the resources available and reading a long list of books, articles or blogs on e-mail tips is the first action you should take if you are experiencing serious problems with excessive e-mails. Instead, three simple choices will go a long way toward solving the problem and getting things going in the right direction.

1. Choose to use e-mail only to the extent *it* serves *you*.

2. Choose to proactively reduce the number of e-mails you receive.

3. Choose to significantly improve your e-mail user skills.

Let's take a closer look at these three choices.

Choose to use e-mail only to the extent *it* serves *you*. This is the ultimate test with any so-called productivity tool. Is this resource serving me or am I serving it? Call it a lifestyle choice, a serious commitment or whatever you prefer. Just make sure you stop complaining about your e-mail problem and start doing something about it. In one sense, you teach what you allow. Stop inviting or allowing people to interrupt you through e-mail. Eliminate the irrational belief that you must be accessible 24 hours a day and seven days a week. Establish reasonable boundaries that create an appropriate amount of time to focus on your top priorities each day.

E-mails are like fishhooks. Imagine a fish swimming around in a lake having a great time. The fish is in control of where he goes and what he does with his time and energy...until he takes the bait and bites a hook. Once the fish gets hooked, the person at the other end of the line is now in control. It just doesn't make much sense to give up control of your time and energy by biting at the equivalent of fish bait, i.e., e-mails, all day long. They say 80 percent of your results come from 20 percent of your efforts. Unless answering e-mail is your top priority, you should consider totally ignoring your e-mail system for at least 20 percent of your day. If you still do not have enough interruption-free time to complete your top priorities for the day, gradually increase your quiet time until you achieve the right balance. Break the habit of going after the digital equivalent of bait that is dangled in front of you each day. Once you make a firm decision to stop allowing constant e-mail interruptions, you can read the books, articles and resources on e-mail tips and discover practical ways to implement your decision. For example, turn off the visual and audible e-mail alerts, use the phone when it is more appropriate, set aside specific blocks of time to process e-mails, etc.

Choose to proactively reduce the number of e-mails you receive. Once you make the lifestyle choice to limit your e-mail use to activities that serve you well, it is probably a good idea to take measures to reduce the flow of incoming messages. Reduce the number of e-mails you receive by sending out fewer e-mails (since the number of e-mails you receive is apparently a function of how many you send) or by limiting your use of the "reply to all" feature. Also, use filters, use a separate e-mail address for retailers and others who might share your address with advertisers, or simply ask people who use your e-mail address too frequently or inappropriately to stop (or block specific users with the blocking function on your e-mail system if they don't take the hint). If all else fails, stop using your old address and establish a new e-mail address and be more careful about how you give out your new address.

Choose to significantly improve your e-mail user skills. Both of the books I mentioned earlier offer excellent advice on how to develop effective and efficient e-mail skills. In other words, how to become a power user of e-mails. They will teach you how to improve the quality of e-mails you send out, how to help those you frequently interact with improve the quality of their messages to you, and how to keep the messages flowing through your in-box properly. For example, Mark Hurst suggests that you focus on quickly and efficiently processing incoming messages and keeping your e-mail in-box empty. Treat your in-box like a computer game. The object of the game is to get better and better at quickly processing your incoming messages and clearing your in-box. You win when you have a totally clear in-box. The point being, e-mail use exploded overnight and is now well entrenched as a communication tool. Most of us have had very little training on how to use this tool. Stop assuming you inherently know how to use this tool and get some training if you need it.

Einstein advised that we cannot solve problems by using the same kind of thinking we used when we created them. The purpose of these three simple choices is to give you a logical framework for beginning to solve your e-mail problems. Since different techniques work for different people and in different situations, one chapter in a book can't address all the possible solutions. I'll keep studying the books, articles and resources, and sharing more ideas related to each of these categories with my clients. Meanwhile, use these three choices to help make sure e-mail is your friend and not your foe.

Nicole Chamblin
Organized Visions
Freeport, New York

917.747.8408
nchamblin@organizedvisions.com
www.organizedvisions.com

Nicole Chamblin, owner of Organized Visions, is dedicated to providing solutions that allow her clients to be more organized.

Organized Visions was born from Nicole's desire to help others reach their goals. She helps companies and individuals make their visions of being more focused and productive a reality. As a professional organizer and productivity consultant, Nicole combines years of problem solving and project management experience with her training in peer mediation and marketing to create simple, yet unique answers for her clients.

Nicole earned a bachelor's degree in psychology, a master's in communication, and is a member of various professional organizations, including the National Association of Professional Organizers New York Chapter (NAPO-NY) and the Network for Productivity Excellence (NPEX). She is a Certified *GO System* Trainer available for workshops, speaking engagements and hands-on consulting.

Nicole lives in Freeport, N.Y., with her husband.

3
Delegation Mastery
Nicole Chamblin

What?

Some people feel the need to totally control everything related to their job. This attitude, of course, leaves no room for delegation and is a proven formula for overloading, stress and job burnout.

Others confuse delegation with passing the buck. They are good at letting go of responsibility, skipping out on work and forcing others to take care of things. These people often bark orders at everyone, let go and hope for the best. That's not true delegation or management; it is irresponsible and incompetent behavior.

True delegation is about maintaining the appropriate balance between letting go and staying involved. In an environment that promotes true delegation, everyone is constantly learning new things and experiencing personal and professional growth. Workplace challenges, and the responsibility and authority that accompany these challenges, flow down the chain of command smoothly and effectively. Everyone delegates work and receives delegated work. Everyone learns. Everyone grows.

So What?

Unfortunately, many managers lay the foundation for their lifelong delegation habits with their first managerial assignment. I'll admit, as a new manager, I often found it difficult to let go of projects. I was used to handling the day-to-day aspects of getting the work done. I didn't view letting go as delegating; I thought of it as giving up control. It wasn't easy to trust that others would manage the projects properly. I insisted on being closely involved in everything to make sure things were getting done. The more that I stayed involved in the daily workload, the more overwhelmed I became. The more overwhelmed I felt, the more I tried to hold on and maintain control over everything. It was a vicious cycle that made transitioning to the role of a new manager extremely difficult. Such behavior usually earns you the title of micromanager...not a great start for a beginner manager.

If you are a responsible person, it's human nature to fall victim to micromanagement as a new manager. Your boss, colleagues and direct reports expect you to think more strategically and to exert more influence over others. You suddenly find yourself attending more meetings with senior management, staff members, vendors, suppliers and clients. (Now, you finally know what happens behind closed doors!) You typically walk into the meetings with plenty of work to do and walk out with even more. Ongoing, day-to-day projects have to stay on task, special projects must be completed, and unexpected issues must be handled. You know how to do much of the daily work with your eyes closed, so when things come across your desk, it is easier to just do it yourself. Unfortunately, in this situation, the easy way out *now* creates significant problems *later*. And when you fail to delegate, it rarely takes long for problems to catch up with you.

A bottleneck begins to develop and old work begins to pile up. New assignments delegated to you during your daily round of meetings soon join the growing pile. Wait a minute...what's going on here? Why are others freely delegating items to you, but at the same time you are hesitant to send them down the line to your subordinates? Why are you the only one that's feeling overwhelmed? Wasn't being a manager supposed to be easy?

Guess what? If you operate like this, you are not becoming a good manager. Failure to appropriately delegate is often viewed by others as overly controlling behavior. In case you haven't figured it out, no one...absolutely no one...likes to work with or for a control freak. If you are a new manager and you want to survive and prosper, don't head down this road. If you are a seasoned manager struggling with delegation because of habits you formed early in your career, mastering delegation might be just the thing you need to re-energize your career.

Think about it. You can wait around and hope that circumstances will somehow provide you with a chance for advancement, or you can take the initiative and proactively create career advancement opportunities for everyone. *Here's a simple strategy for career success. If you want to increase the odds of your advancement, you have to do two things: get your boss promoted and train your replacement.* Otherwise, you will be stuck in your current job for two reasons: there is nowhere to go and there is no one to replace you.

This brings up an interesting point about delegation. Most management books and courses primarily focus on downstream delegation. If you want to maximize your potential for career success, learn to master both downstream delegation between you and your subordinates and *help your boss master downstream delegation to you.* In other words, make sure your boss is very comfortable delegating tasks to you that will stretch your current capabilities and prepare you for greater responsibilities.

Now What?

Mastering delegation is easier said than done. You can read about it for years, talk about it for years...but you are only going to get good at it when you start doing it. Since delegating is counterintuitive (it actually *is* easier to do things yourself and *harder* to teach someone else how to do something and delegate it in the beginning), it will not "come naturally" as they say. In the beginning, you've got to force yourself to delegate and prepare for the possible consequences of putting your fate in someone else's hands. Learning to delegate is like learning a new dance routine, the more you practice it, the more fluid and natural it becomes. Don't avoid learning to master something as important to your career as delegation just because you might get roughed up a little bit when you are learning.

Taking the following steps will get you on the road to delegation mastery:

Step One: Evaluate Strengths and Struggles

Identify your strengths and areas of opportunity as a manager, and evaluate your team members to develop an understanding of their individual strengths and weaknesses. By the way, do not assume because you are the boss that you are the best at everything. If that is the case, you have the wrong people on your team. Recognize that a task that energizes you or one of your staff members might drain the energy of other members of your team. For example, one person may get excited about dealing with details, while others would get burned out. Some people are naturally assertive, while others are naturally accommodating. Some people are precise and methodical, while others are spontaneous and big picture-oriented. *Understanding the strengths, struggles and natural behavior of your team members is a foundational issue if you want to master delegation.* One of your highest priorities as a manager is to really understand the capabilities of your team members.

Step Two: Evaluate the Tasks and Responsibilities Critical to Your Success

Leverage the strengths of your team by *breaking down the jobs to be done in your department and matching them with the best person to do the job.* Following through with the preceding examples, you might assign a number-crunching spreadsheet job to a methodical person on your staff, and a long-term strategic planning job to the big picture-oriented team member. Remember, missed deadlines, poor performance, stress and job burnout may be symptoms of a job mismatch.

Step Three: Begin Delegating with Reasonable Freedom and Boundaries

Be up front and honest with your team members. Tell them you are going to start with small projects to *give them the opportunity to earn more responsibility and authority.* Develop a reporting system that keeps you informed about the progress of the projects, while giving your team leeway to manage their work. Establish reasonable guidelines and expectations that allow them to begin making decisions and taking action on their own. In other words, do whatever it takes to train your replacement and insist that your team members do the same. You will *all* grow as they get used to project ownership and demonstrating that they can be trusted with the responsibility.

Step Four: Prepare for Your Next Job

Now that you are creating opportunities for your team members and lightening your workload at the same time, start getting ready to move up by asking your boss to delegate more responsibility to you. Use your own experience with your staff to convince your boss how much better it is to truly manage a growing, energized group of people, rather than wearing yourself down by trying to do it all yourself.

Here's the big lesson! Another good way to describe a master leader/manager is as a master learner/teacher. If a work unit is structured properly, it is an honor to have a job delegated to you. It means someone trusts and respects you. In life, you tend to get what you give. If you want others to honor, trust and respect you, learn all you can about your job, teach others as much as you can as soon as you can...and then let go and enjoy the benefits of delegation mastery.

Chris Crouch
DME Training and Consulting
Memphis, Tennessee

901.748.1293
cc@dmetraining.com
www.thegosystem.com

Chris is passionate about learning. He has spent years researching and studying both the mental and physical aspects of being organized. He shares his discoveries through books, articles, presentations and training programs. He is president of DME Training and Consulting, author of *Getting Organized* and the developer of the *GO System* training course.

DME Training and Consulting is focused on helping people who are seeking to do things more effectively, efficiently and enjoyably.

4
The Big Three
Chris Crouch

What?

Allow me to get a bit Joyce Kilmer-ish for a moment: "I think that I shall never see, a *number* as beautiful as a 3."

I don't think Joyce would mind me borrowing a line from his poem about trees to help introduce the idea that the number "3" is important to people who feel overwhelmed. Three is a useful number if you are a busy person, a digestible number...it's anti-overwhelming. Three has long been an important number among religious teachers and public speakers, it is important in the fields of art and entertainment, and it is important to people who are struggling with their workload.

My friend, who is a retired minister, told me that he was taught in seminary to design sermons using the "three points and a poem" format. Great speakers have long known the value of designing speeches with three main points. And many movies, TV sitcoms and plays use a three-part or three-act story line format. *Seinfield* often launched three stories in the beginning of each episode and tied them all together by the end of the show. And, of course, there are the Three Bears, the Three Little Pigs, the Three Stooges, the Three Musketeers, the Three Blind Mice, the Three Laws of Robotics (if you are a science-fiction and Isaac Asimov fan), and then there's the big three in school…reading, writing and arithmetic. The list goes on and on…and on.

In terms of triage, the medical practice of properly sorting or categorizing incoming patients in a massive emergency where the lifesaving resources exceed the number of patients needing attention, the number 3 has the potential to save your life. There are many forms of triage that vary slightly. For purposes of this discussion, let's assume the triage physician has been taught to categorize incoming patients as follows:

1. Will not survive even if treated immediately.

2. Will survive even if they are not treated immediately.

3. Will only survive if they are treated immediately.

In case you haven't already guessed, here's where I am going with all this talk about the number 3. Frequently perform triage on your workload; design most of your days so you will get the three most important things you need to get done each day completed before noon.

So What?

Let's talk about the simple psychology related to this strategy. Using this triage technique makes it much easier to decide what to do next. If you have a multitude of things on your mind and a work environment full of projects circling your desk waiting to land, you can easily succumb to the negative effects of choice overload. Here's a relevant quote from Barry Schwartz, author of the book *The Paradox of Choice*:

"As the number of available choices increases, as it has in our consumer culture, the autonomy, control, and liberation this variety brings are powerful and positive. But as the number of choices keeps growing, negative aspects of having a multitude of options begins to appear. As the number of choices grows further, the negatives escalate until we become overloaded. At this point, choice no longer liberates, but debilitates. It might even be said to tyrannize."

Barry's comments also apply to you and your workload. You can become debilitated by choice overload whether you are trying to buy a new pair of jeans, a camera or a car, or trying to decide what to do next at work.

Now What?

Use the triage technique to design your morning activities and then shift down one more gear and get into a binary decision-making mode (the opposite of choice overload). The term binary means, "consisting of two parts or two separate elements." If it is before noon, you simply *compare any potential distraction – e-mails, phone calls, drop-in visitors, etc. – with the most important unfinished item* on your list of three important things to get done for the day. It is much easier to compare competing demands on your time and make a decision if you are comparing two things, rather than trying to constantly juggle a multitude of things. This system also allows for the fact that something may come up that is more important than any of the three things you thought were most important. If that should happen, ignore the original three items until you complete the unexpected important task. Only become concerned about doing this if you begin to notice a pattern of frequent, unexpected items. Repeat the process in the afternoon or work in a totally unstructured manner. Do whatever works best for you. I personally think there is a lot of value in having plenty of unstructured time.

Consider setting up a "triage" hanging file in your desk drawer – take three minutes at the end of each day to jot down the three most important things you have to do the next day, and then drop the list of three items into the triage file and go home.

You may think getting three things done each day is a bit wimpy. However, I didn't say you only had to do three things a day. I am simply suggesting that, at a minimum, you get three very important things done each day before you allow other less important forces to take control of your behavior. Ideally, by concentrating, focusing and minimizing distractions early in the day, you will finish your triage items and have plenty of time to continue your focused efforts. Or, you can join the masses in the world of the overwhelmed, if that is your preference.

I'll admit, when I get my triage items done some days, I like to screw around awhile and piddle with the work equivalent of shiny objects that attract my attention. However, I find that if I am honest and rational about what I put on my triage list, I feel very good about what I accomplish most days. For example, I am almost finished writing this chapter and it's not even time for lunch yet. Finishing this chapter ended up on my triage list since one of the roles I have defined for myself is being an author.

This brings up another important issue related to joyful and productive living. *Maintain a long-term vision and a short-term focus*. My long-term vision is to publish and sell books. My short-term focus related to that vision is to write one thing at a time and turn it over to my publisher to see if she can turn it into something with a cover, pages and a price tag. This short-term focus stuff won't work too well if you don't have a clue about your long-term vision.

In a way, writers are lucky. When you define yourself as a writer, your long-term vision and short-term focus are easy to determine. Writers write. If you don't write most days, you are probably not really a writer. Now that I think about it, it is probably a pretty good idea to see if you can come up with a one-word description of your main focus. That would mean that sellers sell, managers manage, leaders lead, teachers teach, inventors invent, and so forth and so on. Using sellers as an example doesn't mean they sell all the time. However, it does mean they sell most of the time and, hopefully, they sell some each day. It also means that activities related to selling should be the kind of items most frequently dropped in their triage file.

I know life is not always this simple, but keeping things simple is a good idea when you are trying to establish a reasonable level of order in your life. In reality, some days I am a teacher and items related to teaching belong in my triage file. Some days I am a vacationing spouse and parent. On those days, items related to watching the sunset from the beach, eating shrimp and taking my daughter to get Hawaiian Shaved Ice belong in my triage file. Life balance is the ultimate trump card when considering your triage list.

That's all for now on this topic. Admit it, some of you didn't know Joyce Kilmer was a guy, did you?

Sue DeRoos, CPO
Organize U
Macomb, Illinois

309.837.3802
sue@organizeU2.com
www.organizeU2.com

Sue DeRoos enjoys seeing the positive impact that being organized has on people's careers, relationships and personal self-worth. She believes that having the right tools is the first step toward successfully building anything, including an organized life.

Sue has built a career from her passion for organizing. In 1997, after 20 years in the business world, she established Organize U. As a trainer, speaker and productivity consultant to individuals and companies, Sue provides her clients with the tools and knowledge they need to build more balanced, productive and focused lives.

In addition to being president of Organize U, Sue is a member of the Network for Productivity Excellence (NPEX), National Association of Professional Organizers (NAPO) and American Society of Training and Development (ASTD). She is also a Certified *GO System* Trainer and the National Organizing Consultant to California Closets, Inc.

5
The Price of Procrastination
Sue DeRoos

What?

"I've got to stop procrastinating and get something done about that!" Sound familiar? It's a phrase we hear in many different ways:

- "I'm so busy right now; I'll get to it later."
- "I'll do it when I find the time."
- "I'll do it right after I finish this."

Oh…the possibilities!

Studies show that at least 95 percent of us occasionally procrastinate. We don't really need a study to understand that procrastination is a widespread problem. In fact, we *all* procrastinate at times. It's human nature to put things off. That's not a big problem. It's like putting off doing your laundry. It creates minor problems at first. But, keep it up and it becomes a major problem, unless you don't mind wearing dirty, wrinkled clothes. Pull the same stunt with work priorities, relationship issues, health issues, etc., and watch your troubles quickly pile up!

Procrastination means, "putting off doing something until a future time; postponing or delaying needlessly." It is something that plagues most of us at times whether we realize it or not. As I mentioned, occasionally putting something off might not immediately create problems, but when it starts to negatively impact our work performance, family relationships and health, it's time to take action. It's time to stop procrastinating and do something.

Procrastination, of course, is not a new problem. Leonardo da Vinci was a man of incredible talent and, yet, rarely completed a project on time. He finished painting *The Last Supper* only after his patron threatened to cut off all funds. Another master procrastinator was Samuel Taylor Coleridge, the famous 18th century poet. During his life, publishers constantly mentioned impending pieces that ultimately failed to appear. Although these men were successful, can you imagine what they might have accomplished with the discipline to overcome their tendency to procrastinate? We'll never know.

If you listen to advertisers and read their advertisements, it is truly amazing that procrastination still exists at all in our society. You'd think with all the latest technological discoveries, gadgets and conveniences, such as computers, cell phones, PDAs, the Internet, microwaves, drive-through restaurants, drive-through cleaners, drive-through coffee shops, etc., we'd have plenty of time to quickly take care of everything and lounge about for the rest of the day. For some reason, things don't seem to be working out that way.

So What?

So, what are you putting off? What's keeping you from tackling those important tasks? What is procrastination costing you?

Procrastination can certainly result in financial costs such as late fees, penalties or higher prices due to last-minute decisions…but what about the nonfinancial costs? In business, putting off completing a task until the last minute not only creates unnecessary *current stress*; it probably means the quality of your work will be compromised. This creates *future stress* when your career potential stagnates or declines due to late, low-quality work. Once again, little things may not matter that much at first. Maybe you will get away with procrastinating on a few little things. However, big projects are simply an aggregation of smaller tasks and projects. If you develop the habit of procrastinating on the little things, sooner or later the big projects will fall apart…along with your career. One of my clients finally decided to stop procrastinating about getting organized only after his doctor told him his health was at risk due to excessive stress, much of it caused by his lack of organization. That's a pretty high price to pay for putting things off.

Now What?

Let's keep things simple! Procrastination is about *not* doing things. Therefore, the logical antidote to most procrastination problems is to *do something*. Try using a few of these simple tools to quickly turn things around.

Acknowledge the problem and evaluate the cause. Acknowledging that you are procrastinating, and knowing what's stopping you from starting or completing a task, is a great first step if you want to solve the problem of procrastination. You can't fix something if you don't know it is broken, or solve a problem if you don't know it exists.

Procrastination can be caused by unproductive or self-defeating thought patterns, such as:

- Avoiding difficult, frustrating or boring tasks
- Lack of clarity or direction...not knowing how to get started
- Feeling that the task is pointless
- Fear of failure
- Perfectionism
- Believing that people work better under pressure

At the extreme, procrastination caused by fear of failure, perfectionism and other forms of psychological baggage or self-defeating behavior, might require the help of a therapist. However, often there is no deep, psychological, underlying root cause of procrastination. Many people in our achievement-oriented society procrastinate because they simply take on far more than they can accomplish in a given time frame. Or, too many fun and interesting alternatives (TV sitcoms and reality shows, movies, computer games, hobbies, etc.) are competing for their time, energy and attention. Identifying *why* you have been procrastinating is often key to solving the problem and getting things back under control.

Define the scope of the problem. Remember elementary school, when things got a bit chaotic? The teacher would make you line up in an attempt to restore order. Do the same thing with all your chaotic, unfinished tasks. Line them up! Make a list of them...or even better; write each thing you have to do on a 3 x 5 index card. Just the act of writing everything down makes most people feel better and more in control. When they do this, some people are often surprised to find that things are not as bad as they thought.

Break down projects and tasks into manageable steps. Most of us think of our projects in terms that are too big! Think about the project of building a house. You can't pour the foundation, put the hardware on the cabinets and decorate it all in the same day (unless you are on ABC's *Extreme Makeover: Home Edition*). If a project seems too big, break it down. All major, overwhelming projects can always be broken down into a series of minor, digestible projects. Create new index cards for these new tasks.

Stop making excuses and identify what *must* be done. For some reason, people rarely procrastinate when it comes to making excuses about procrastinating. I guess excuses make them feel better about putting off the *inevitable*. Surprisingly, classifying things as inevitable is one of the first things you should consider if you are struggling with procrastination. Ruthlessly attack your deck of index cards and eliminate anything and everything that cannot be honestly classified as *inevitable* or *unavoidable*. If you are a typical procrastinator, this action will quickly eliminate 80 percent of your burden. Vilfredo Pareto (the 80/20 Rule guy) taught us this around the turn of the 19th century. Remember, we get 80 percent of our results from 20 percent of our efforts.

Be clear about what has to happen and in what order. Take a look at all of the remaining tasks you've listed on your index cards. Select the most important task and place it facedown on your desk. Now, pick the index card with the next most important task and place it facedown on top of the other card. Keep this process up until all your index cards are facedown and in one stack. Turn the stack over. Congratulations! You have now prioritized your workload and established a blueprint for getting it done.

Get to work. Schedule one-hour blocks of time to work on the tasks represented by your stack of index cards. Use a timer. Set it for an hour...pull the top index card and get to work on the task listed on the card. Focus your total attention on the task. Take no phone calls...allow no interruptions! Maintain this discipline for *at least half* of your workday until you get your workload under control. It is unrealistic to do this for the *entire day*. Expect the unexpected. Be flexible in emergency situations. Just don't let unexpected issues consume your entire day...every day.

You are not going to end procrastination altogether. This is an unrealistic goal if you are a normal human being operating in today's work environment. A life without any procrastination is not likely, but as Christopher Parker (an English actor) remarked, "Procrastination is like a credit card: it's a lot of fun until you get the bill." By using the tools described previously, you can be on your way to building a life of getting your work done on time, making a good living, enjoying life...and paying your bills! What are you waiting on? Get started now!

Pat DeSanto
DeSanto Resources
Helmetta, New Jersey

973.766.2931
pat@desantoresources.com
www.DeSantoResources.com

Pat DeSanto is passionate about empowering her clients:

"When we struggle with disorganization and low productivity we can feel overwhelmed and out of control. We can feel as though we've failed. I teach my clients how to turn that around, create repeatable success, and be proud of what they do."

As an author, public speaker, Certified *GO System* Trainer and consultant for the *Paper Tiger* software, Pat has been making a difference in her clients' lives since 2001. She brings 20 years of business and education experience, along with degrees in science and communications, to her work with companies and groups of all sizes.

Memberships in the Network for Productivity Excellence (NPEX), the National Association of Professional Organizers (NAPO), the Northern New Jersey Association of Professional Organizers, and local learning and development groups, provide Pat with the powerful resources she brings to her clients.

6
The Fifth Sound
Pat DeSanto

What?

Music is a powerful tool. I, like many productivity and organizing professionals, often play calming music while working with clients. With music as our harmonious guide, our efforts often take on a rhythm and balance that helps us accomplish great things. Music reduces stress, increases focus and raises spirits.

Some years ago, I met someone who shared my love of music, but with a twist. His love was barbershop music, also known as singing a cappella in four-part harmony. I knew about four-part harmony, but not barbershop harmony, so I decided to learn about it. I had no idea how much this new experience would teach me about productivity and organization.

As I listened to the four-part harmony, I noticed another sound. Rising from the voices of lead, tenor, baritone and bass, I heard an additional fifth resonance. Everything else seemed to be a part of this sound, and it was *growing*. I later learned that this phenomenon, known as the "expanded or fifth sound," is created when each quartet member produces his part of the harmony accurately and consistently. This resonance is the watermark of barbershop harmony.

My "aha" moment, however, didn't occur until I attended my first quartet rehearsal. I realized there was a powerful connection between what I was hearing and my quest to be more productive. The singers created an organic, palpable energy larger than each individual voice. I recognized this as the same type of energy I work to create with my clients. By applying focus, intent and skill, my clients and I often expand our mindset and increase our energy. Some call it being in the "zone," which results in increased workflow, clarity of purpose and peak efficiency. We literally become *unstoppable*.

So What?

Everyone has the potential to create this highly productive and enjoyable energy. Although some people rarely experience this harmonious state, many seem to be constantly searching for it. Clients struggling with disorganization and disharmony tend to view *all* their efforts as ineffective. However, when I meet with them, I often see evidence that things aren't so bad. I see a combination of smart choices and not-so-smart choices. So what happened? What prevents some people from achieving harmony at work and enjoying operating at their peak level?

Frustration and impatience in disharmonious situations cause people to hop from one project or strategy to another, giving each little time to produce results. At best, any results are fragmented and short-lived. Imagine our quartet singers for a moment. What would happen if they each decided to sing a different song or sing in a different key? You would hear singing, but if each member of the group failed to pay attention to the details of a particular song or key, there would be no balance or harmony. It would probably sound more like noise than music. Even the best individual voice cannot overcome the discord within the group in such a situation.

The same thing often occurs if you try to use several "sure thing" productivity solutions that have no relationship to each other or your particular situation. When your efforts are sporadic and uncoordinated, it is difficult to achieve harmony. Only by applying balance, consistency and focus, can you create the synergy, and energy, of the fifth sound.

Now What?

Take a few minutes and think about your past. Can you remember a time when you felt unstoppable? When you knew just what to do and did it without fanfare or hesitation? *My philosophy is this: If you can do it once, you can do it twice. If you can do it twice, you can do it all the time.*

Let's look deeper into the fifth sound. Clearly, producing this sound requires certain ingredients that make up the overall "package of performance." In barbershop music, this package would include:

1. Four voices separate and, yet, complimentary to each other.
2. Each voice performing different and distinct notes.
3. The right blend of resonance and volume.
4. The repeatable execution of chords that affect the overall performance.

We can do the same with your day-to-day routine by looking at how this relates.

Barbershop:	Four voices separate and, yet, complimentary to each other.
You:	Several day-to-day activities such as speaking on the phone, conducting research, working on projects and meeting with others...all happening separately, but supporting the same goal.
Barbershop:	Each voice performing different and distinct notes.
You:	Each task with its own criteria, deadlines and complexity.
Barbershop:	The right balance of resonance and volume.
You:	Applying the correct amount of time and focus on each task.
Barbershop:	The repeatable execution of chords that create the fifth sound.
You:	The repeatable execution of actions and decisions that create work harmony and synergy.

Now it's your turn. Think about creating a fifth sound in your workplace. It's easier than you think, because you've already done it! To do it consistently, however, we want to begin with a few smart strategies. Our barbershop quartet can lead the way.

The lead in the quartet is the easiest one to hear. He carries the melody. So let's start with what you need to hear most...*tell yourself the truth.* There is no point in attending classes or buying books on how to master keeping your files in order if you hate filing and won't do it. Take stock of the productivity issues you *want* to tackle and which ones you will resist to the end. Some office activities can be delegated to others more open to that task. If you can't delegate, however, it is even more important that you identify these problem areas so you can use extra care in finding friendly systems or products that will help you follow through, and feel good about it.

The tenor sings his part of the song above the lead. At times he must step out of his comfort zone to sing the highest notes in the register. Follow his example and step out of your comfort zone to *evaluate what is effective and why*. Make a list of what you've tried and a few short phrases for each item to clarify. For example:

> You took a memory improvement class and put Post-it notes on everything in your office. Did it help? "For about a month." Then what happened? "I forgot to buy more Post-it notes."

Some things just won't fit your work style or personality. By separating the good ideas from the bad ideas now, you don't have to waste time on those choices later.

The baritone is next. He sings in a range between the voices of lead and bass. He must know when to alter his voice to a higher range to complement the lead and when to lower it to support the bass chords. You can do the same by *being flexible* and willing to adapt to your situation. This, of course, implies that you remain keenly aware of the overall goals of your organization, or the project or task you are working on, and determine how you might need to adjust when necessary to create a successful outcome.

The bass might fool you. His voice can sound simplistic as he maintains the lower range of the song. Well, who said simple was bad? In a complicated world where solutions can sometimes create more difficulty than the problems they are supposed to fix, *simplicity is the key*. The bass is the anchor of the quartet. The anchor provides stability so that, no matter what happens during the song, the three other singers can always return to the sure and steady guide the bass provides. Keep your solutions easy to learn, easy to maintain and repeatable, and no matter how busy you are or how many surprises you encounter, you will always have a sure and steady guide to help you regroup.

We all know that life has many ups and downs. Often, when you settle into that peaceful and easy flow of work, something disorienting seems to happen. The tempo of your work will accelerate, the volume will go up and you will either adapt to the new situation or lose control.

Remember your musical guides:

- Tell yourself the truth.
- Evaluate what works for you and why.
- Be flexible.
- Keep it simple.

I told you music was a powerful tool! You can be powerful too. The fifth sound is waiting for you. Try it on. Take it for a spin, but hold on.

Your fifth sound will surely emerge... and then it will *grow*... and then, so will *you*.

Barb Friedman
Organize IT
Milwaukee, Wisconsin

414.351.8420
organizeit@wi.rr.com
www.organizeitbiz.com

"Being organized is a learned skill," according to Organize IT Owner and President Barb Friedman. Barb consults with individuals and businesses to increase productivity and reduce stress.

Barb has been teaching workshops on organizing, time management and prioritizing since 1998. Building on strengths and compensating for weaknesses, Barb works with her clients to create systems that work in the real world. Her proven tips and techniques have been featured in a wide variety of national newspapers, magazines and television shows.

As a Certified *GO System* Trainer, member of the National Association of Professional Organizers (NAPO), and a founding member and past president of the Wisconsin NAPO chapter, Barb continues to pursue education in her quest to find the right solutions for her clients.

Through humor, motivation and knowledge, Barb will put you on the path to living the life you want. Don't agonize...Organize IT!

7
Choose Your Habits Carefully
Barb Friedman

What?

Remember when you were a youngster and your parents always told you to get dressed, make your bed and brush your teeth? And this was all before breakfast! These were the "house" rules. Then, at school you had to follow "school" rules such as, be at your desk and in your seat when the bell rings, turn in your homework in the container labeled "homework," and have your pencil and paper out and ready.

Grown-ups were so bossy! As kids, we didn't like it, but we knew we had to do certain tasks every day. By the time we entered adulthood, something amazing happened. These repetitive "tasks" became habits and routines! We didn't think about these tasks…we just did them.

Many of the routines we learned as children still drive our behavior as adults. We still automatically get dressed, brush our teeth and eat breakfast before we leave for the day. We just go to work instead of school.

All habits seem to fall into two main categories: Habits that help you and make life better, and habits that hinder you and create problems in your life. Unfortunately, it is often hard to tell which is which.

So What?

What do habits have to do with being focused, organized and productive? Everything!

Let's say you have developed a habit that is quite common these days...taking your cell phone with you everywhere you go. When you do this you are, in effect, proactively inviting interruptions. When your cell phone rings (or makes whatever noise you have programmed it to make when someone calls you), it is human nature to either answer it or want to answer it. Either way, you are distracted and your attention is diverted from whatever you are doing to something else.

According to experiments conducted in 2001 by Joshua Rubinstein, Jeffrey Evans and David Meyer, when your attention is diverted, you go through two stages during the switch from one area of focus to another: 1) goal shifting and 2) rule activation. During goal shifting you mentally decide, "I want to do *this* instead of *that*." Different tasks are also driven by different sets of mental rules. Therefore, during the rule activation stage, you go through the process of "turning off the rules for *that* and turning on the rules for *this*." The bottom line according to Meyer: "Even brief mental blocks created by shifting between tasks *can cost as much as 40 percent of someone's productive time*." In other words, seemingly insignificant interruptions, like a ringing cell phone or beeping e-mail device, *can cost you up to 100 days of productive time each year*. First of all, this is a high cost for accessibility and also, who really wants or needs to be accessible all of the time? Although it is a popular idea these days, being accessible all the time is an inherently bad idea. There are many reasons it is a bad idea, but at a minimum, it can significantly impact your productivity and drain your energy.

The human nervous system has a built-in feature to help you "rise to the occasion" when you find yourself in an emergency situation. This feature is commonly referred to as the fight-or-flight response. It evolved to help you handle *short-term* emergency situations (such as being chased by a saber-toothed tiger). When you sense danger, real or perceived, your body jolts into action and prepares you to handle the crisis. Pay particular attention to the fact that I said the feature was designed to help you deal with *short-term* emergency situations.

Here's the point, the human body is an energy-producing and energy-using entity. If an excessive amount of energy is being used to power the fight-or-flight processes, there will be little left over to allocate for other uses. Therefore, if you are perpetually in the fight-or-flight mode, you will often feel drained of energy.

Let's summarize this and see what we can learn from it.

- Being accessible *all the time* is the equivalent of an ongoing, long-term emergency situation and uses a tremendous amount of your energy.

- Humans were not designed to have their fight-or-flight system continuously activated. The saber-toothed tiger chased them and it was over, or the human escaped and things settled back into a normal routine. The tiger didn't chase them eight, 16 or 24 hours a day. Most emergencies that activated primitive man's fight-or-flight system were over quickly…one way or another.

- If you choose an ongoing lifestyle that generates ongoing stress, you will consume a significant amount of energy and lose track of what needs your attention now.

- Many extremely counterproductive events *are often triggered by fairly innocent-looking bad habits.*

So, we are back to where we started…some habits help you and make life better, and some habits hinder you and create problems in your life.

Now What?

Let's sort through some of the more common, modern-day habits and see if we can find some practical ways to allocate more energy to your healthy lifestyle and less to your emergency alert systems.

- Cell phones and other electronic communication devices are great. They can save you time and make you more productive – if they are used properly. However, for the sake of your overall survival, disconnect from them on a regular basis (at least a few hours every day at work and whenever possible during your leisure time). In other words, the most important feature of all your electronic devices is the on/off button.

- Constantly rushing, in whatever form you choose to do it, is a bad habit. Sure, you have to pick up the pace sometimes. Just make sure picking up the pace does not morph into an ongoing lifestyle choice.

- Sleep is the mother of all restorative processes. Determine how much you need (it varies among individuals) and get enough every night.

- Avoid any situation that calls for you to be constantly accessible. If you are human, you need some down-time...every day!

- If you notice an ongoing pattern of stress and chaos in your life, *do not allow the pattern to continue*! Consider it as a strong signal from your environment that you need to do things differently. This is the essence of the course I teach to help people get more focused, organized and productive. I simply help people form habits that naturally minimize or eliminate chaos and stress and free up more energy. For example:

  - Do you know how to develop habits that help you manage any project from beginning to end and create the results you desire effectively and efficiently?

  - Do you know how to develop habits that allow you to quickly prioritize your work?

  - Do you know how to develop habits that allow you to establish the proper volume and pace of your workload?

  - Do you know how to recognize and change unproductive habits?

When you were a youngster, your parents chose most of your habits for you. Now that you are an adult, you have to determine which habits you should develop and nourish and which ones need to go. It's a simple message that can make a huge difference in your life. Stop inviting the modern-day equivalent of saber-toothed tigers into your life (enough of them will show up on their own without your assistance). Choose your habits carefully!

Janice Gentles-Jones
The Productive Workplace
Westbury, New York

516.333.6578
info@theproductiveworkplace.com
www.theproductiveworkplace.com

Janice Gentles-Jones is an author, speaker and productivity enthusiast. She has over 11 years of experience educating busy professionals on how to use technology efficiently, and how to make the most of their time, space and information. Her workshops are custom-tailored to meet her audiences' needs.

Janice helps her clients reduce work-related stress so they have more time for revenue-generating tasks. She enjoys helping others achieve their goals and gets personal satisfaction from the success stories of those she helps.

Janice holds a master's degree in instructional technology from New York Institute of Technology, and a bachelor's degree in political science from Queens College. She led the training and help desk departments at a large New York pharmaceutical firm for seven years, and has trained more than 6,500 people over the span of her career.

Janice is available for speaking engagements, in-house training, consulting and custom workshops.

8
The Technology Myth
Janice Gentles-Jones

What?

OK, I admit it. I am a technology junkie. I *love* technology. Some women covet shoes, some fancy chocolate...I love any gadget that can help me get or stay organized. When new software or hardware is released, I often read about it and then visit the store to see how it looks, feels and smells. I know it may sound strange to some of you, but it's what I love to do. However, as much as I love technology, before buying it, I determine how it will impact my current productivity. I want to know exactly how it fits into my life and my work situation. Like many busy professionals, I cannot afford to use a tool that reduces my productivity...no matter how many bells and whistles it may have or how many promises the advertisers make about how great it is.

So many technology tools on the market today are touted as the next best thing for people who desire to get more organized and productive. But are all the promises really true? Many companies invest in PDAs, Treos, Blackberrys and instant-messaging devices...technological devices all too familiar to most busy professionals. But do these tools really make us more productive? Some believe the myth that all new technology makes us more productive. Some people avoid technology because they fear it may make them less productive. As usual, the truth lies somewhere between these two extremes.

So What?

Unquestionably, technology has changed the way we work today. A relatively short time ago, our primary follow-up activities were returning phone calls or answering the mail. Now, in addition to live phone calls, we must respond to voice mails, e-mails, text messages, pagers and various other forms of communicating with technology. It's amazing what we sometimes accomplish in such a short time by using technology. But there is a downside...technology has made many people instantly and constantly accessible. This instantaneous and ongoing accessibility can be devastating to your productivity and ability to live a reasonably balanced life.

If you are like most people these days, it's important to have processes, systems and habits in place to manage the incoming flow of information. These systems and habits should allow you to easily receive, process, follow up on or store information. Unfortunately, many people impulsively buy the hottest new technology gadget on the market and assume it will somehow fit in with their current workflow processes and systems. Even worse...they are struggling because they have no well-defined workflow processes and systems and they buy the gadget hoping it will stop or minimize the chaos in their life. *Here's a good guideline for selecting and using technology: Design good workflow processes, systems and habits first, then buy the technology to support what you have designed.* Otherwise, there is a good chance the chaos in your life will increase instead of decrease.

For example, when I recently worked with a vice president of human resources on a consulting project, I was amazed by how often we were interrupted by e-mail alerts, instant messages, her ringing Blackberry and calls coming in on her regular business phone. Each time an alert on one of these devices sounded...a ringing phone, a visual alert for incoming e-mails or a beep for text messages, she would stop and look at them. This, of course, constantly interrupted our workflow. I asked her how she got any work done with the constant distractions. She said it was very hard and that she often worked an extra three to four hours, after business hours, due to all the interruptions. The devices still interrupted her in the evenings, although less frequently, so she was at least able to get some work done after regular business hours. The problem was further aggravated by the fact that most of her days were filled with meetings. Her company uses Microsoft Outlook and co-workers can electronically invite her to meetings. The meetings appear on her calendar as part of her schedule unless she removes them. For some reason, she felt compelled to accept all the invitations, so before she knew it, her day was filled with back-to-back meetings. When I asked to see her calendar, she had no empty time slots over the next few days. My client was rapidly losing control of her day (and life) due to unproductive use of technology.

- Is there any hope of staying productive in an environment of constant technological interruptions?

- Can technology really make life easier for us?

- Are the benefits of using technology simply a myth?

Well, I am happy to say that yes there is hope. There are systems we can put in place to help us properly manage technology and positively impact our productivity.

Now What?

Let your productivity needs drive your technology, don't let technology drive you. Here are some suggestions to help you stay productive and use technology appropriately.

Set clear goals, both professionally and personally.

Without clear goals for your day, you will likely default to the barrage of distractions and interruptions that prevent you from achieving the things that are most important to you. Without goals, it is difficult to make sound decisions on how to allocate your time and energy. Is immediately accepting every phone call, e-mail, text message, etc., your most important work goal? I doubt it. No matter how many technological devices you possess, each day should include an appropriate amount of quiet, uninterrupted time for focused concentration on your highest priority or priorities.

Teach people how to best communicate with you.

Tell your colleagues or staff how you make decisions and how you prefer to receive information that requires you to make a decision. Encourage them to use your preferred method of communication if they want a timely response from you. Be sure to follow through on your word if you want them to respect your guidelines. For example, many people now have a business phone, home phone and cell phone. It is difficult to keep up with voice mails on all three lines. Specify one place for important voice mails and use the other phones for outgoing calls only. Teach people to use this phone line for all incoming voice mails. Over time, people will get used to calling your primary "message line" if they really need you to respond quickly.

Ask the question, "Can this request wait?"

Ask this question (even if it is a silent question to yourself) every time you're interrupted. Apply this method to people, e-mails, phone calls, instant messages, pager alerts or anything else that interrupts your planned activities. Get out of the habit of reacting to the incoming barrage of digital interruptions. *In general, if you are interacting face-to-face with another person, assume that paying attention to them is more important than responding to an unknown caller, e-mailer, text messenger, etc.* Develop a reputation for following up promptly. A good follow-up reputation, even when you must postpone a request, keeps some people from designating everything as urgent.

Schedule specific times during the day to check e-mails and voice mails.

This gives you more control over your workday. The key is to use this time wisely. Not every e-mail must be acted upon immediately. *Try not to work on the e-mails as you review them.* Look through all of them quickly before you start to work on any of them. *If an e-mail requires your attention, schedule it into your overall workload like any other project.*

Turn off visual and audible e-mail alerts.

Alerts, as their name implies, are very distracting. It's human nature to look at the message when you see or hear an alert. As mentioned previously, schedule specific times to process such items.

Learn the capabilities of your technological resources.

The fact is, technology can save us a lot of time and make life so much easier – if we know more about how to properly use it. I know of people who have worked with a specific software program for years wishing for an easier way to perform a certain task…and they finally discover there was a built-in feature that could handle the task in a few clicks. Attend training classes, watch video demonstrations or hire someone to help you learn the capabilities of your technological resources. This will also help you determine which features fit your work preferences, work style and your personality.

Take it from a technology lover. Set your goals, define your system for managing your work and incoming items, understand how your technology works and then use it to support your goals when appropriate. Don't get overwhelmed by the very gadgets that are there to help you get things done. Remember, you drive your technology, don't let technology drive you.

Kimberly Guay
A Clear Vision Organizing &
Productivity Consulting
Danville, California

925.984.9181
kimguay@aclearvisionorganizing.com
www.aclearvisionorganizing.com

Kimberly Guay is owner and founder of A Clear Vision Organizing & Productivity Consulting. She has 20+ years of financial services experience, including strategic planning, product development, project management, marketing, online services, vendor management, contract negotiation, and training and human resources development. She has held senior executive positions at several banks, has been a speaker at national conferences and has been a project management consultant.

A Clear Vision provides productivity coaching and organizing solutions for busy executives and workplace professionals. They offer workshops, seminars, and one-on-one consulting and ongoing support. Their mission is to find simple and effective solutions for clients to maximize their productivity, and to enable them to reduce stress and get more enjoyment out of their work and personal lives.

Kim is professional development director for the San Francisco Chapter of the National Association of Professional Organizers (NAPO). She is also a member of both the American Society for Training and Development (ASTD) and the National Study Group on Chronic Disorganization (NSGCD).

9
Setting Boundaries
Kimberly Guay

What?

You've spent the last four Saturdays at the office. You check your calendar, see the upcoming long holiday weekend and think, "Great, I can come in on Monday when no one else is here and actually get some work finished, uninterrupted." How did you get to this place?

The answer could be because you allow people to interrupt you and bump your key priorities, or because you attend meetings that drag on when you need to work on time-sensitive projects. Sometimes it's your boss who expects you to be available for phone calls or projects while you are on vacation.

Some companies tolerate behavior that most of us think is inappropriate, but why do we personally let ourselves get pushed beyond our boundaries? Are we afraid of being accused of not being a team player, being uncooperative, or doing just enough work to get by? Maybe it's fear of reprisal or lack of self-confidence.

So What?

Enjoying personal time is crucial to maximizing your performance. Whether you enjoy a particular hobby, travel, time with your family, exercise, or time to rest, think and reflect, personal time allows your physical being to recharge and re-energize.

The boundaries you establish in your work environment will: a) allow you to be more productive, making a greater contribution to the company's success and profitability; b) allow you to work fewer hours; and c) improve the quality of your life and reduce stress.

If you use normal work hours as productively as possible, you'll rarely need to give up personal time. Setting work boundaries in these three key areas will help you gain control over your work schedule and productivity:

- Avoiding time wasters
- Turning down unreasonable requests
- Stopping inappropriate behavior and comments from others

Now What?

Try the following techniques to help set reasonable boundaries:

Establish boundaries *before* you start a new job. When interviewing with companies, endeavor to discover as much as possible about the company's culture, values, ethics and habits, and how these align with your own values.

Look at companies where leaders demonstrate healthy boundaries. In a recent TV interview, John Thompson, chairman and

CEO of Symantec, said that he does not take his Blackberry with him when he goes on vacation. Neither is he compelled to check his e-mail at night or on the weekend. John says, "You ought to be able to find some balance, somewhere in your life...I believe we all need to be refreshed and we should have hobbies that allow us some form of mental escape." Symantec's revenue, under John Thompson's guidance, has gone from $630 million in 1999 to over $5 billion today.

The power of a soft "No." Protect your schedule and learn to say no without alienating others. Block out time on your calendar to work on specific projects and don't allow disruptions during that time. If someone wants to schedule a meeting at that time, offer an alternative: "I can't meet then, but tomorrow at 10:30 a.m. would work." If your boss makes the request, be diplomatic. Let him or her know that it may impact another important deadline. Ask for input in determining priorities.

Find a way or a place to concentrate. The "open-door" policy advocated by some leadership books is not always appropriate. If it will help you concentrate and stay focused, close your door at times. If you work in a cubicle, post a note that you are working on a critical project and indicate when you'll be available. If possible, move to a conference room for a couple of hours. If you can telecommute, work at home on a certain day of the week, or for specific projects.

Be open, likable, empathetic and supportive...but whenever possible, maintain your closest friendships with people outside your work life. Share intimate and personal details with the people who love you, and have no vested interest in your work performance, relationships and issues. Ask yourself how you would feel if the information you shared were broadcast throughout the organization.

In her book, *The Secret Handshake: Mastering the Politics of the Business Inner Circle*, Kathleen Kelley Reardon, Ph.D., writes, "You have to know whom to trust with information. Friendship complicates things because it brings with it certain obligations to share information." I'm not advocating that you be someone you're not, but fewer intimate relationships at work minimizes the temptation to discuss something with a co-worker you might later regret.

Decide on language boundaries. Think about your tolerance for off-color jokes, offensive language and verbal bullying. Most companies have policies that prohibit these behaviors, but in reality, we often tolerate them. If these situations occur, you could ignore them, join in or laugh them off, but be aware that these actions might come back to haunt you.

To tackle emotionally upsetting situations, authors Katherine Crowley and Kathi Elster, in *Working with You Is Killing Me*, recommend a technique they call "unhooking." Unhooking allows you to gain control of a situation by changing your emotional reaction and then stating your boundaries or requirements in clear, factual terms.

Have an exit strategy for unproductive meetings. If a meeting's purpose is just to communicate information, ask if an e-mail recap can be sent instead. Let the meeting organizer know what time you need to leave. If you called the meeting, prepare an agenda, ask participants to do as much prework as possible, bring any reference material needed, start on time, and stick to the agenda and the time limit. Minimizing the invitee list often helps.

Decide how many hours, and when, you will work. We all have project deadlines or phases in our careers when we have to put in extra hours. You may have international clients that require early or late phone calls. Decide what time you will arrive at work and what time you will leave, and keep to your schedule.

If you are getting all of your work done in a normal workday, don't let peer pressure compel you to stay longer than you need to just to fit in. Trying to keep up with other workaholics is a thankless challenge.

Protect what you do on your own time. Don't allow peers or others at your company to minimize, denigrate or interrupt your personal commitments. If you are involved with volunteer work or your children's school or sports events, schedule that time on your calendar just as you would an important work commitment.

Be very specific with your staff, co-workers and boss that you will not check your e-mail, voice mail, pager or Blackberry while on vacation. Set up your voice mail announcement and e-mail out-of-office auto reply with your date of return, and do not check messages until that time.

Another area that we often sacrifice is sleep. Sleep is underrated. William Dement, M.D., Ph.D., calls us a "sleep-sick society." He attributes chronic sleep deprivation to many medical and health-related issues. Don't leave sleep just for the weekend. Make sure you get adequate sleep during the week. Fatigue can completely undermine your performance and you may not even realize it.

Don't let other people give you their monkeys. Some people are notorious for trying to get others to take on their projects or responsibilities. They try to "put the monkey on your back."

You might be someone who feels responsible for other people's monkeys. Stop! Allow people to solve their own problems and deal with their own monkeys.

If you are ill, stay home. Don't feel guilty for staying home when ill. Exposing your co-workers to illness can jeopardize the entire department's productivity. The best thing you can do for your company is to take care of yourself. A colleague ignored some troubling symptoms for months due to a large, high-profile project. By the time she had a checkup, she was diagnosed with a stage four cancer.

Don't let your own guilt bully you. Perfectionism drives some people beyond reasonable boundaries. You can't work enough hours in the week to do everything perfectly. The myth – "If it's worth doing, it's worth doing well." – does not apply to everything. Trust your own judgment; make sure you understand your boss's priorities, your own priorities, and how your contributions impact the success of the company.

Make changes gradually and carefully in your current position. If you want to make some healthy changes at your current position, identify the specific steps you want to take. Write out a list of issues to change and start with the one that gives you the greatest benefit.

Make your changes gradually. New boundaries may be confusing to people around you. Talk with your boss about your goals, and ask for his or her help in making the changes. Talk with your peers and others in your work group. When setting a boundary with someone, state your needs without anger. Be respectful, specific and brief.

Setting boundaries can be difficult, especially if your co-workers are not used to you doing it, but the payoff in terms of increased productivity, quality of life and reduced stress, are well worth the effort.

Nancy Hagan
Effective Executive, LLC
Maineville, Ohio

513.899.9949
Nancy@EffectiveExec.com
www.EffectiveExec.com

Nancy Hagan is a certified executive coach with over two decades of experience in the business world. She works exclusively with executives, business owners and managers, and is dedicated to helping clients implement simple, yet powerful systems that quickly impact efficiency, productivity and profitability.

Nancy is a member of the National Association of Professional Organizers (NAPO) and the International Coach Federation (ICF), as well as a *Paper Tiger* consultant and a Certified *GO System* Trainer. She is also a professional speaker and conducts seminars and workshops throughout North America.

10
Designing Your Day
Nancy Hagan

What?

Do you feel overwhelmed with the demands of the day? Are you at the mercy of whatever comes up, unable to find time to focus on the high-priority work that would move your business and life forward?

How can you create a comfortable balance with all you have to do?

So What?

Reduce stress, improve productivity and increase peace of mind by *Designing Your Day*. "But, wait," you may be thinking. "I don't want to be boxed in, rigid, in a straightjacket!" Of course not! The good news is you really can have the best of both worlds – freedom with a solid foundation.

It's your very own custom plan, including spontaneity and time for you! It will be much better than being scattered and overwhelmed – and easier than you think. You may have many of the components already in place. *Designing Your Day* can optimize your time, energy and results!

Now What?

Consider these ideas to simplify the process of *Designing Your Day*.

Set up a grid or spreadsheet that represents the time available during a seven-day period. Block out each day in 30-minute increments of time (or print out a "Reality Check Time Grid" worksheet at www.EffectiveExec.com/realitycheck.php).

Block out time for your essentials and customize with choices that are vital to your progress. These blocks of time might include:

- Focus time (High-quality time for your most important tasks.)
- Thinking and planning
- Breaks (Scheduling time every hour or so for standing, stretching or a few deep breaths can make a difference.)
- Energizers (Include things in your day that you love to do and enhance your energy. These may be outside work.)
- Phone calls
- Meetings (Be selective, avoiding as many as possible.)
- Reading
- Processing mail
- Processing e-mail
- Commuting
- Meals
- Sleep (Studies show too little sleep negatively impacts productivity.)

Look at the most important things to be done each week – things that give you the highest return on time invested. The 80/20 Rule says 80 percent of your results typically come from 20 percent of your activities. Spending 20 percent of an eight-hour day (just over 90 minutes) on your highest priorities will give a substantial return. Take care to identify the critical 20 percent that will create the maximum impact. Ask yourself:

What moves your business forward?
What moves your life forward?
Where can you best use your strengths?

Group similar tasks and create "designated days." It's easier and more efficient to go from one task to another when you're already in that mode. For example, tasks like project work, client prep, writing, client time, phone calls, meetings and appointments, etc., can be grouped together to get them done more efficiently. "Designated days" let you *focus on what's really important for large blocks of time.*

Decide the best place and time for each activity. Consider these factors:

Environment. If a quiet place that provides uninterrupted time is hard to come by, you may want to try one or more of these strategies:

- Put a sign on your (closed) door indicating the time when you will be free. For example, "available at 3 p.m.," like professors' office hours.
- Use an empty conference room.
- Go to the library.
- Wear a special hat to let your team know you are focused on a high priority.

- Develop a workplace culture of honoring an hour or two of uninterrupted time. Watch everyone's productivity and morale improve!

Energy level. Don't waste your best energy on a low-energy task (like going through most e-mail). And don't set yourself up for diminished results by scheduling a critical task that requires your best when your energy is winding down. Work with your energy patterns:

- High-priority and difficult tasks when at your best.
- Secondary and easy things, like phone calls and e-mail, later in the day when your energy is waning. Open mail near the end of the workday, but do deal with it! Today's unprocessed mail is tomorrow's pile!

Create modules in your day – windows of opportunity – to help you balance all the things you want and need to do. These modules should be blocks of time designated for focused attention. Consider starting with 30, 60 or 90-minute intervals. Modules keep you on track with your goals and help create balance. They make it easier to adjust how much time to spend on any particular task, and help you remain realistic with your choices. You can still be flexible. You are ultimately in charge of your life! Modules are moveable. Stay with your structure if possible, but be flexible to accomplish what you want. Examples of module activities include:

- Thinking and planning
- Writing
- Projects
- Client work
- Prospect follow-up
- Meetings

- Weekly or monthly planning
- Administrative (tying up loose ends)
- Phone calls
- E-mail (five minutes in the morning for time-sensitive e-mail only, such as a change of appointment; afternoon for routine matters)
- Mail
- Resting and relaxing

Schedule these blocks of time for your most important responsibilities. These blocks of time should be focused time, which means no e-mail, phone calls or interruptions. That's vital to achieving your goals. Just start, even if you don't feel ready. You'll find it gets easier each time and gives you a real productivity boost! We don't find time. We must *make time*, or it won't happen.

Schedule only 50 percent of your day to allow for the unexpected. If unexpected events do not occur, you will have bonus time for additional priorities.

Designate a block of time to take care of "naggers." Those things that nag at you every time you see them ("Take care of me! You know you should! You never get anything done!"). Often they are little things, such as the pile of mail or the phone call to correct a problem. Once you give them attention, they usually take less time than expected, yield wonderful relief and a sense of accomplishment, and won't nag you anymore! Bigger things (such as updating a manual) can be whittled away week by week. For example, spend 30 minutes to an hour on larger projects, and then don't worry about them until the next time comes around. To *prevent* naggers from accumulating, use the two-minute rule. If it takes two minutes or less – just do it!

Eliminate everything that isn't vital to the vision of your life, and especially anything that conflicts with it. Is attending one more committee meeting or surfing the net more important than the time you need to achieve your most important goals? Real satisfaction comes from doing the things that are truly important.

Every day, include things you love to do; and every week, include things you want to do, but never get around to! Don't wait for someday. Life happens now!

Adjusting Your Day

Once you have your patterns established, you will want to adjust for comfort and/or changing circumstances. You may want to keep a simple "cue card" of your basic design for quick reference. List the days of the week and the special tasks for each day on a 3 x 5 index card and keep it handy.

So what if things don't go according to plan? That's life, and that's the beauty of "designated days." We will never get everything done (sorry to burst that bubble). Wait until the "designated day" comes around next week and do it then, unless it's truly urgent. But *Designing Your Day* makes those emergencies less frequent. Your mind can let go in the meantime, because you know the time is coming when it will get done. Or, maybe you will realize it isn't how you want to spend your precious time.

You won't always adhere to your plan. Life happens. But you now have a framework with guidelines to remind you where you want to be. Like the painted lanes on the highway, this framework will help keep you on track. Of course, you may decide to take the next exit for some good reason, or just because you need a break. But it will be a more conscious choice. You will want to continually evaluate and make adjustments. *Designing Your Day* will make your choices more apparent.

Final Touches

You may want to have little rituals to complete your day at the office: planning tomorrow's work, clearing your desk, backing up your files, etc. Think of what you would like to accomplish, how you would like to feel, what would help you get there, and build them into your day.

Designing Your Day allows you to capitalize on you at your best, taking care of your needs and wants, and elevating your quality of life! Be kind to yourself. We are not machines! Skills improve with experience.

Someone once said, "Time isn't money. Time is life!" Are you getting the most from yours by *Designing Your Day*?

Ann Michael Henry
Mise En Place
Victor, New York

585.924.8470
annmichael@m-e-p.com
www.m-e-p.com

It is no surprise that with a passion for cooking, Ann Michael Henry named her organization and productivity consulting firm after a cooking term. The firm's name, Mise En Place, means "setting in place." The term is used to describe preparation done before starting the actual cooking process. So, what does this have to do with being organized and productive?

At Mise En Place, the overarching philosophy remains the same, but the ingredients, tools and processes change to accommodate a client's personal work style. The right mix of ingredients and tools is applied to transform disorganization into a manageable, streamlined process that stimulates creativity and meaningful productivity. To Ann Michael, her work in organization and productivity consulting is like putting a gourmet meal on the table...Magnifique!

Ann Michael is a consultant for the *GO System* and *Taming the Paper Tiger®*, a founding member of the Network for Productivity Excellence (NPEX), and a member of the National Association of Professional Organizers (NAPO). She also offers various webinars and workshops on improving organization and productivity.

11
Spontaneity
Ann Michael Henry

What?

It's amazing what a new day can bring. Just when you think you have the day all planned out, something unexpected happens. Living in upstate New York, winter brings many of those unpredictable moments, and today was no exception. I awoke to discover that there was more snow on the ground; a blanket of white fluff covered the landscape. Earlier this week, spring was in the air; new streams and puddles had formed in my yard, birds chirped excitedly, including the squawking of the geese returning north, and a lone crocus eagerly popped its head out of the damp soil ready to add color to the dreary winter palette. As I write this, the fluffy white blanket is back, and I am heading out with my trusted old shovel, ready to tackle my driveway yet again! One minute it is a perfect spring day, the next minute temperatures return to single digits – how quickly it all can change. Oh, how I so enjoy the spontaneity of it all!

I certainly hadn't planned to shovel the driveway this morning – a 45-minute task at least! The interesting thing is that I feel wonderfully refreshed and rejuvenated. I was able to accommodate this blip; an unexpected event – although one would argue that snow in March could never be considered unexpected! It's not going to throw off my day. If anything, I'm more excited about facing the tasks in front of me. Why? Because I did something unplanned, something that was fun and energizing, and something different from the ordinary daily routine. Yet, I can quickly get back to my priorities for the day without missing a beat.

So What?

How many times have you had the opportunity to take advantage of something different or something that you love to do, only to find you had to turn it down because you already felt so overloaded? Or, worst yet, you are presented with the opportunity and you are expected to do it, to add it to an already huge pile of responsibilities. For most of us, the ability to do something we enjoy or something new is just what we want – a change of pace. How sad is it that this sense of excitement is accompanied by such a draining feeling?

Unfortunately, I see this "letdown" all too often in my clients' lives. Something new comes in and it triggers a feeling of foreboding instead of excitement…just one more thing to do, when it should be viewed as an exhilarating release from the monotony of our daily lives. We begin to ask ourselves, *"Will I ever get a break from this routine?"*

Take one senior executive that I work with. We began working together because she wanted to stop feeling so overwhelmed. She was looking for a better way to manage her responsibilities so she would have time for "other" things. We implemented a number of strategies including a new paper management process: a tickler file, effective use of e-mail and improved delegation skills for administrative tasks. She understood that changing habits was what it was all about. She also realized that changing habits isn't always easy and opted for ongoing check ins to keep the new habits in check.

We had been working together for several months and she was making great progress. Then I arrived one morning for our work session and sensed that something was a little off. There were a few piles on her desk, and the table she used for her projects was completely covered. Clearly, she was in the midst of something big. Well, you know the feeling when the boss gets up from the desk, walks to the door, closes it, turns, sits back down and pauses...you know something is up, you can feel it in the air. This was one of those moments.

Client: As she points to her tickler system she says, *"I don't think this is working for me. I've got this 80-hour project that came in and it will demand all of my time. In the meantime, none of that* (again pointing to her tickler system) *is getting done...it's just sitting there, staring at me. What good is that?"*

Me: *"This 80-hour project is your top priority?"*

Client: *"Yes, it's a great business opportunity."*

Me: *"Before we worked together, how would you have handled your workload and this opportunity?"*

Client: *"My regular work would have taken a backseat, it would have waited."*

Me: *"And now, you take the time to gather up everything that comes in, assess what the next steps are, when they need to be done, and integrate this into your process, correct?"*

Client: *"Yes."* (Showing a faint smile.)

Me: *"With this strategy, you know where everything is and what needs to be done. That's different than six months ago, isn't it?"*

Client: *"Well... yes."* (A sense of calm begins to return.)

Me: *"So, what I'm seeing is that you have clarity about what needs to be done. Prioritization has happened, there is a sense of order and your ability to focus has improved dramatically. Now, for the first time, these new habits are being challenged by a **spontaneous event**."*

Client: *"Correct."* (A quizzical look comes over her face.)

Me: *"I think you've done an excellent job! You immediately focused your efforts on your top priority, this key business opportunity. It seems to me that the processes we've put in place have allowed you to do just what you wanted to do – be responsive to business opportunities as they arise, and* (gesturing to the tickler system), *when it's time to get back on track and pick up where you left off; you'll be able to do so without missing a beat. You know exactly where everything is and in what priority you will need to tackle it once business gets back to normal. It looks as though your new strategies are working just fine."*

Client: After a long pause to contemplate, I get that look of "OK wise guy, you were right!" With a smile on her face, she says, *"Yea, OK...let's get to work."*

This was the first time she had encountered spontaneity since changing her work habits. She was befuddled as to how to handle it. Having created a work environment that was organized, focused and productive, she was startled when she was thrown a curveball. Startled in a different way, however. In the past, when something popped up, chaos would ensue. That was how she was used to reacting. When this didn't happen, she immediately kicked into the mode of *my new system isn't working, just like my old system didn't!* In reality, this was a test of the new system. Could it handle an unexpected event?

The good news is she quickly saw how the environment we had created served as an automatic "reboot." It allowed her to focus on high-priority, spontaneous events...and then return to her responsibilities with a sense of control and confidence, knowing what her next steps would be. When I returned a few weeks later, the 80-hour project was complete and business had returned to normal.

She shared several observations and conclusions with me:

- It was easy to get back on track after the unexpected project. In fact, major progress on a number of other items had been made since then.

- She could successfully and confidently incorporate spontaneous opportunities into her everyday workload.

- She didn't have to give up those things that gave her comfort – the paper calendar, the occasional small pile on her desk, the ability to spread out on her worktable to tackle a project.

- A lot of the things she thought she should do really weren't important.

There was an air of energy and excitement in the office that day!

Now What?

So, how does one go about being able to accommodate (and enjoy) spontaneity without spiraling out of control? Interestingly enough, in the case of this senior executive, it boils down to only two key habits.

Habit #1: Establishing a "command post" (e.g., a tickler file system) for all of the information coming her way was crucial. Now, whether it's e-mail, voice mail, paper, verbal requests or her thoughts, they are all captured in one centralized location. Bottom line, she knows where everything is. Items are no longer scattered on multiple lists, sticky notes or bouncing around in her head like popcorn.

Habit #2: Anything new that comes her way is greeted by one of five decisions:

- Can this information be discarded?

- Can I delegate this?

- Can I take immediate action and move this item out quickly?

- Does this information belong in a reference file?

- If action on my part is required, what is the next action I need to take, and when will I take it?

If the incoming item has not already been processed by the time she gets to the last question, the item is added to her command post. It could end up in today's file or some time next week, or even next month or next quarter. Now, when a high-priority, spontaneous opportunity presents itself, she turns to her command post, assesses the next several days workload, asks those five questions again, re-prioritizes accordingly, begins work on the new opportunity (now the No. 1 priority), and returns to the command post upon completion – confident in the fact that she knows where everything is and what comes next.

Indeed, she is accomplishing her objective of being able to handle everything coming at her. She is ready to take on the next spontaneous event!

Christine Kominiak
Productive Sense Training &
Consulting
Corrales, New Mexico

505.890.4607
Christine@ProductiveSense.com
www.ProductiveSense.com

Christine Kominiak teaches people how to get more done with less effort. As the owner of Productive Sense Training & Consulting, Christine provides consulting services, seminars and workshops across the country.

Christine is certified as a *Paper Tiger* Authorized Consultant (PTAC) through Hemphill Productivity Institute, and is a Certified *GO System* Trainer. She teaches people how to get and stay more organized and productive by addressing several major issues that cause chaos and disorganization.

She is a member of the Network for Productivity Excellence (NPEX), Albuquerque Area Professional Organizers (AAPO), National Association of Professional Organizers (NAPO), and the Albuquerque Hispano Chamber of Commerce.

12
The Power of Clarity
Christine Kominiak

What?

In the years I've worked helping individuals and groups improve their productivity, I've consistently observed that people often get quite excited in the beginning of a project. Sometimes that excitement translates into a smooth beginning and the project gets under way. Unfortunately, as the project unfolds and the details become overabundant and complicated, frustration creeps in and dampens some of the initial enthusiasm. This frustration often peaks midway through a project, and for many people the option of walking away seems far more appealing than following through and completing the project. In this situation, the ability to maintain enthusiasm and consistently follow through on what you started separates the superstars from the mediocre players in life.

The key to project closure and success is clarifying what you want, being specific about how you are going to get it, and taking the next best step...one after another...until you fully accomplish what you set out to do.

So What?

Like many people, I didn't go into business to be a salesperson. I went into business to pursue my interest in teaching and helping others. Of course, I expected to make a decent living pursuing this course of action. Admittedly, in the beginning, I embraced the irrational belief that clients would somehow show up, I would help them improve their productivity, they would pay me for my assistance...and I would live happily ever after. Even though I knew I should proactively contact prospects, and understood what I should do to develop business, I didn't enjoy the process and would often put it off. At first, I didn't even realize I was procrastinating on this critical issue. I would rationalize that something else, anything other than making a sales call, was more important and devote excessive amount of time and energy to less important issues. I was very good at developing what is sometimes referred to as avoidance strategies. It was easy to rationalize that responding to low priority e-mails, working on my Web site or focusing on other low-value tasks was more important than something I didn't enjoy doing. After all, I felt busy...I felt like I was working hard...actually, I was working hard. When I finally acknowledged my sales call reluctance, I made a firm commitment to follow through and master the process of sales and business development.

For years, I have understood the value of breaking a large project into small tasks. In fact, I even used helpful tools like a project management table, my planner and my tickler file to break projects into smaller, more digestible pieces. However, for some reason, I wasn't consistently following through on certain planned tasks related to sales. Forcing myself to work on certain tasks through the use of willpower only worked for so long. On an intellectual level, I understood the importance of the tasks and how they fit into the big picture of building my business. However, after the newness of my commitment wore off, I found myself putting things off as usual.

As I was evaluating why my new commitment and new plan wasn't working, I was introduced (one of those seemingly coincidental or synchronistic events that frequently occurs when you get more focused) to the simple concept of *clarity*. *Sometimes when your plans to achieve your goals are not working, you simply need to clarify your goals or clarify your specific plans to reach your goals.* The granddaddy of self-help books, *Think and Grow Rich*, by Napoleon Hill offers a wealth of good advice for anyone determined to accomplish significant things in life. One of the recommendations in the book specifically addressed my situation. Paraphrasing the recommendation: *Adopt a definite purpose and develop definite steps to achieve your purpose.*

I realized it wasn't enough to decide that I wanted to increase business, or to put a reminder in my tickler file to "call prospects," I had to come up with something more specific...more definite. According to Napoleon Hill, I had to specify the exact amount I desired to earn, exactly what I would do in return for this amount, the exact date I intended to possess the money, and the exact steps I would take to achieve my plans. So I decided to make my plans more definite...to clarify what I was really going to do!

For example, I decided that to increase my sales to the level I desired, I would set a goal of conducting a minimum of two training sessions per month with at least 15 participants. This specific goal translated into the minimum profit I desired at that stage in the development of my business. In my mind, this was a very reasonable and achievable goal.

Because I knew how many participants I desired in my classes, I knew what size companies would likely have this many potential participants. That, in turn, allowed me to identify specific companies in my market area to prospect. That, in turn, made my networking and prospecting efforts easier, since I now knew to look for people who worked for those specific companies or had connections to those companies.

Next, using some assumptions, I computed that if I contacted three qualified prospects every week and told them about my training class, in a year's time that would result in achieving my goal of conducting a minimum of two classes every month. Of course, my computations reflected the fact that not all of the companies I contacted would hire me. So, all I had to be concerned about was making three calls every week. Since I had already "done the math," I simply had to execute my plan.

Then, I decided what I would say to the prospects or networking contacts to get a conversation started. I anticipated the potential responses and determined how I would handle each of them (including determining that they might not be a prospect for my services and moving on to the next prospect on the list).

As I executed my plan, I continued to learn, adjust and get more specific about what I would do every day to generate sales. Interestingly, as I got more specific about how I would generate the sales (i.e., gained more clarity), the sales process began energizing me rather than draining my energy. I discovered that the process I previously dreaded and avoided was becoming more interesting, mentally challenging and stimulating. Being clear and being specific turned my mental attitude around. I had discovered one of the simple secrets to accomplishing great things. *The secret can be articulated in one word...clarity.*

Now What?

Of course just understanding all this intellectually won't get the job done. There are many ways to gain clarity. Here are a few specific ideas to help you convert your intellectual understanding into practical action.

The Salami Concept

Years ago, I learned about the "Salami Technique" (mentioned in the book *Doing It Now* by Edwin C. Bliss) from my friend and colleague Dr. Meggin McIntosh. Summarizing the idea: If for some strange reason you decided to eat an entire salami, it would probably be a good idea to slice it up and eat it one bite at a time. By slicing up the specific steps to reach my sales goals, I was easily able to determine my next action and the logical sequence of actions. Had I not broken the steps into small, digestible bites, I likely would have continued to focus on low-value tasks or avoidance strategies.

The Power of Specifics

You cannot "do" a goal. You can only "do" specific activities that will result in the accomplishment of the goal. The more you clarify your goal, the easier it is to determine the specific steps that will result in the achievement of your goal. It sounds almost too simple to be true, but if you are stalled on a project...stop any further action (including your procrastination) until you determine the important specifics. Keep it simple and be more specific about:

- What you want.

- How you are going to get what you want.

Although I mentioned that this solution seems too simple to be true, it is interesting to note that when questioned in a Harris Interactive Survey of 23,000 employees, only 37 percent of the survey participants said they had a clear understanding of what their organization was trying to achieve and why. Once again...do the math...this means 63 percent of the people surveyed lacked clarity!

Leading a Horse to Water Concept

In their book *Following Through*, Steve Levinson and Pete C. Greider suggest that contrary to popular belief, if you lead a horse to water...it certainly may not drink it. However, getting the horse close to the water makes it easier and more likely that it will take a drink. Another way of looking at this idea is that by separating the easy part of the project from the hard part, you'll move closer to your goal and be in a better position to maintain momentum and get the job done. Once I started "leading the horse to water" and creating less daunting, more specific tasks, I found myself following through more consistently.

Like most things in nature, the human nervous system has a maximum capacity. When your workload exceeds your available time and energy, your nervous system is designed to respond in one of three ways: fight, flight or freeze. If you are in the fight-or-flight mode, it is easy to confuse frantic motion with constructive action and fill up your day with low value or meaningless activities. If you respond by freezing, all follow-up and progress comes to a halt. If you find yourself in any of these situations...remember *your next best step is to simply seek clarity.*

Kay Kotan
Get Organized!
Kansas City, Missouri

816.350.0333
kay@getorganizedKC.com
www.getorganizedKC.com

Kay Kotan is the founder of Get Organized! in Independence, Missouri. She spent 12 years in the corporate banking world before stepping into her entrepreneurial role as a business owner in 1995. Kay has lived in the Kansas City area for the past 22 years, been married to her husband Bob for 14 years and has a son, Cameron, who is 11 years old.

Get Organized! specializes in helping corporate clients identify and solve organizational and productivity challenges. Through coaching and training, Kay provides her clients with systems and processes to become more focused, organized and productive. Her keen eye for quickly detecting productivity issues is key to her success.

Kay is a member of the National Association of Professional Organizers (NAPO) and the Network for Productivity Excellence (NPEX), as well as a certified corporate trainer for the *GO System*.

13
Daddy's Unhappy Overachiever
Kay Kotan

What?

Can you feel the familiar sandpaper scratchiness of his cheek as he gives you a big hug when he comes in the door from work? Can you see the warm, loving smile on his face as a prideful tear rolls out the corner of his eye? Can you hear the words of pride and praise bubbling off his tongue? What? You can't? Really! Well, I confess, neither can I! So your dad may not have been picture perfect. Picture perfect was always my dream, but never my reality.

As children and sometimes adults, some of us long for memories of a proud, caring father. But in these days of divorce and single parenting, those days are often more of a dream than reality. We can't change the past. However, it helps to understand how those parent-child experiences (or lack thereof) shaped us. What can we learn from these experiences? How can we grow from this adversity?

So What?

Well this "daddy's girl" responded to adversity by becoming an overachiever. If I made straight A's he would spend more time with me. If I excelled in sports, he would come to my games. If I behaved perfectly, he would invite me to his house. If I sent the nicest cards on his birthday, Father's Day, and holidays, he would call me. If I had the lead in the school play, he would make arrangements to stay in town to see me perform. If I made National Honor Society, he would show up at my graduation. Maybe some of you had a similar experience.

Come on! Get real! It's not about you! Maybe your dad was just doing the best he could when you consider his life circumstances at the time. Was it good enough for me? Absolutely not! But, that's the hand I was dealt. Like some of you, I chose to respond to my life circumstance by becoming daddy's little overachiever.

For those of you who made a similar choice, in case you haven't noticed, overachieving is very hard work! Sure, we end up with plenty of stuff to proudly display on our resume and talk about at class reunions, but we also end up feeling empty. We continue our father-child drama as grown adults by spending our lives trying to be what we believe others want us to be so we can get what we want from them. And all we really want is unconditional love. The kind of love you get from someone who expects nothing in return. So we spend time chasing our tails being do-gooders and rarely slow down long enough to realize we are living an unauthentic life. We live a frustrating life of trying to meet the expectations of others rather than focusing on who we are and what *we* want.

Unfortunately, when we finally realize we may never be able to please daddy, we sometimes expand our approval-seeking behavior to other areas of life and other people. For example, we might expect our spouses to be everything that dad (or mom) wasn't. If anyone exhibits personality traits similar to our parents, we revert to the mentality of a 7-year-old child and, once again, feel abandoned and unloved. When our best friend forgets our night out, we have flashbacks of being alone on holidays. When our boss doesn't praise us for a job well done, we feel unappreciated. Sometimes we respond to our feelings of inadequacy by overeating, drinking excessively, taking drugs (illegal and prescription) or becoming a workaholic; or by developing anger management issues, anorexia, bulimia, digestive problems, migraines, ulcers, sex addictions...or by overachieving.

While we are running around overachieving and pleasing others, we never really search our souls to discover our true gifts – gifts that are unique to us, gifts that will make us feel grounded, centered and comfortable in our own skin. We rarely find our true calling in life because we are too busy trying to figure out what others want from us or what we have to do to get what we want from others. We then forfeit our own personal peace of mind and joy.

Now What?

Am I happy about my childhood disappointments? No. Is it a good life strategy to let these disappointments continue to drain my energy as an adult? No. Being productive is about living in the present and being energized. Your energy should be allocated to your current life...to the present...not to the past. It takes a lot of soul-searching and self-love to finally figure it all out. But, as stated in *The Contented Achiever: How to Get What You Want and Love What You Get,* "If you want to truly create the life that you deserve, you have to design your play or drama and not get caught up in the drama of others."

In other words, figure out what makes you tick – not what you think others want your tick to sound like. Don't focus on fixing others! Figure out what gives you total joy. What makes you look forward to today? What makes you feel content? What leaves you giddy with happiness?

Create an Adult Family

Get totally engaged in your present life, and totally engaged in creating a caring and supportive adult family. Yes, we are all automatically members of a biological family as children. As an adult, the good news is we can create a new nonbiological family. We can choose who we want to spend our time with during our remaining time on this planet. In the long run, spend most of your time with people who are uplifting and supportive.

Take Good Care of Yourself

Eat a healthy diet. Get some exercise. Get plenty of sleep. See your doctor for your annual checkups. Pamper your soul with meditation or prayer.

Spend Time Getting to Know Yourself

Spend some time journaling. Sometimes what comes out on paper is insightful, surprising and delightful. Reflect on previous journal entries to see if particular people or events trigger negative feelings. If so, explore healthy boundaries and strategies to nurture better relationships with these people and events. Search your heart and soul for the people and things that truly give you boundless joy.

Create New Life Tapes

Don't let thoughts of not being worthy or good enough go on any longer. You are here for a glorious purpose. God intended you to be right here, right now. Think of any negative memories or tapes as what they are...relics of the past that serve no useful purpose in the present. Start creating new memories and tapes that support a life of joy and abundance.

Recolor Your Picture of Daddy

You may need to compare your expectations of daddy with reality. Were your expectations too high? Or, was daddy just not there? Regardless, concentrate on the times (if there were any) when life with daddy was good. If you can't find any good times, think about another father figure in your life who might have stepped up to fill in a few times. As I mentioned before, your biological family is not always your only true family. Count your blessings! Don't get stuck in the past.

The bottom line...my passion is helping people live more organized, productive and joyful lives. My personal experience taught me that it is difficult to build such a life when you are entangled with past memories that are still consuming much of your current life energy. I also understand the dilemma of trying to escape the illusion that a life of overachievement is a good life or a rational way to respond to past disappointments. Overachievement should never be viewed as a viable strategy for creating a joyful, successful life. Let go of any past regrets and any unproductive responses to your past experiences, and begin creating a new life and a new life path that make your remaining days...the best days of your life.

Mary Kutheis (kooth-ice)
Open Spaces, LLC
Workplace Productivity Group®
St. Louis, Missouri

314.313.4996
mary@openspaces4me.com
www.openspaces4me.com

In 2000, after 17 years in the corporate world, Mary established her consulting practice, Open Spaces, LLC – Workplace Productivity Group. Mary candidly admits to being a reformed disorganized person and uses this unique perspective, along with her corporate management experience, to understand and resolve the productivity challenges her clients face.

Mary has developed a keen insight into human behavior and uses this expertise to teach people how to make positive change happen – and make those changes stick. She works with clients to pinpoint areas for improvement, develop action plans to create desired results, assess progress along the way and, ultimately, achieve outcomes that can be measured in improved performance and increased profitability.

A member of the National Speakers Association (NSA), she received her degree in speech communications from the University of Missouri-Columbia. She lives in St. Louis with her husband, son, three dogs and a rental cat.

14
Organization Ain't Oatmeal
Mary Kutheis

What?

We live in an instant-breakfast, instant-message, instant-answer, instant-results kind of world. If there is a way to do things faster or get results sooner, we want it. People selling books, DVDs, CDs, gadgets and even pills rake in millions of dollars telling people how to get rich, get smart, get married, get thin or get organized...right NOW! *Why wait? You can buy things that deliver optimum results in an instant with just the swipe of a credit card!* Or, so they say.

Closely correlated with this kind of thinking is the notion that being physically busy is a measure of your worth as an employee or human being. I'm not talking about the digging ditches kind of physically busy, but the kind of busy that translates to filling every second of the day with activity. For example, making and receiving phone calls while driving, booking your day solid with back-to-back meetings, conducting working lunches every day, or spending small bits of free time throughout the day reading work documents or responding to e-mails and voice mails. These things can certainly serve to keep you busy...but often at the expense of taking the time to sit and think, plan and work intelligently. Some people apparently believe that in order for something to be considered meaningful activity, it must always be observable, physical activity. By this standard, simply sitting quietly in your office and thinking about important issues does not qualify as a productive use of your time. So when are you supposed to do this? When, during a typical workday, are leaders, managers and key employees supposed to slow down and think?

So What?

When people fall prey to quick-results strategies and fill their days with unceasing busyness, their more complex priorities often languish untouched on to-do lists. Such people usually default to tasks that are easier to accomplish or tasks that can be done faster...despite the fact that many of these easier, quicker tasks are relatively unimportant. Moving quickly through the day makes some people feel as if they are making progress, but these people end up paying a steep price for adopting such behavior. How do you want to operate? *Do you want to be a master of busyness or a master of things that really matter?*

If improving personal and professional productivity is your goal, it helps to accept the fact that true organization won't be achieved in the same span of time it takes to cook breakfast oatmeal. Most instant or quick fixes cannot stand the test of time. There are certainly things you can do in a day or an hour to make significant progress on a specific task related to being better organized. But in the end, lasting, long-term, positive results will only come from taking the time to embrace sound organizing principles, learn sound organizing habits and learn to use sound organizing tools. This means thinking about your situation and asking yourself the right questions, creating a plan based on your answers to these questions, executing your plan and maintaining your new organizing habits over time.

Now What?

As mentioned previously, you need to ask yourself some questions in order to pinpoint where your initial improvement efforts should be focused. The following list suggests seven tools, processes and systems that are vital to organizing success in almost anyone's situation. Take the time to think about these comments and questions. Once you get these seven issues in order, you will have created a strong foundation to build on, and you will be in a much better position to tackle some of the more complex organizing issues you might be facing.

1. **A calendar.** Paper or electronic, matters not. What matters is what works for you. Don't be swayed by what works for others. There is nothing antiquated about using a paper calendar if it works for you in your environment. If you choose to use a sophisticated electronic calendar or scheduling program, that's fine. Just make sure it is serving you well. At a minimum, using it should be easier than using a pencil and a paper calendar.

    Questions: Does the calendar you've chosen work for you? Why or why not? Is it serving you or are you serving it?

2. **A contact database.** Names, phone numbers, addresses, etc., must be easy to store and retrieve. Relevant information about contact interactions (how recently you've been in touch, the nature of the contact, etc.) can be invaluable. Do you have a way to capture contact information and easily get it into your database?

Questions: Is your contact database all that it needs to be? Does it support your business goals? Are you keeping up with the important people in your life?

3. **A method for handling incoming items** (five different types of items).

   a. Paper/mail
   b. Phone calls/voice mail
   c. E-mail
   d. Things other people ask you to do
   e. Things you think of that you need to do

Collectively, these items commonly make up a person's to-do list. And while a long list of "to-dos" on a sheet of paper is the method some people use, it has its drawbacks.

Question: Do you have a sound, airtight process for capturing and processing incoming items?

4. **A method for prioritizing your work.** No matter how much you have to do, you can only effectively do one thing at a time. You must have a foolproof method for determining which of your tasks is the highest priority and, further, you need a method for reassessing your priorities throughout your workday as things change and new issues come up.

Questions: Do you start each day with a clear plan for what you need to do first? Can you quickly reassess and re-prioritize when necessary?

5. **A system for handling current projects.** While multitasking on the job is not a good idea, staying on top of multiple projects, simultaneously, is a necessity. You need to have ready access to project information and it needs to be in a form that supports the way you prefer to work.

   Questions: Do you have a designated place for all projects in progress? Do you use an electronic, paper file or binder system and is it working for you?

6. **A reference filing system.** A reference filing system is for papers you may not access on a daily basis, but want to have nearby in case you need to refer to them...hence the name. Interestingly, studies show that we only retrieve 20 percent of the things we file. But since we don't know which 20 percent that's going to be, we file more than is actually necessary. Some issues that will impede filing efforts are not having enough filing space or not knowing what to name a file to find it later when needed.

   Question: Do you have a reference filing system that allows you to easily file things and then easily retrieve them when you need them?

7. **A place for archived files.** Archived files are records and/or documents that you must keep for historical or legal purposes, but the likelihood is small that you will need to access them. Usually archives are not kept in individual offices due to space limitations. A central filing room or off-site storage is more practical.

   Question: Do you have a method for archiving your records?

So, what are your options if you've pinpointed a weakness in one or more of the preceding seven areas and need to come up with solutions? You can:

- Ask around. Pose the challenge to colleagues and get feedback on how they solve the issue in their office or workplace.

- Enlist the help of an organized administrative support person who can brainstorm with you. Remember, it's not about doing things their way, but about collaborating to create methods that work for *you*.

- Read books and articles on organizing topics or work with an organizing/productivity consultant. You'll find suggestions and the names of some particularly good consultants right here in this book or on the following Web site: www.npex.org.

Thinking through the seven processes and the questions posed will give you a tremendous head start on creating an office environment that will support, rather than limit, your ability to get organized and stay organized. There is actually an excellent reason to make instant oatmeal. Use the time you save making the oatmeal to think about how you are going to change things *today*, and begin escaping the illusion that busyness and speed equate to self-worth and importance. You don't have to think about it this instant, take your time! Eat your oatmeal first.

Julie Mahan
Simply Organizing, Inc.
Indianapolis, Indiana

317.865.3172
julie@simplyorganizing.com
www.simplyorganizing.com

As a professional organizer and the owner of Simply Organizing, Inc., Julie Mahan provides productivity services for corporations, nonprofits and small businesses. She helps clients become and stay more organized.

Julie is a member of the National Association for Professional Organizers (NAPO), the National Speakers Association (NSA), the American Society of Training and Development (ASTD), and is a Certified *GO System* Trainer.

The philosophy at Simply Organizing is that organization equals productivity and productivity equals peace of mind. By offering simple, practical applications and examples, Simply Organizing allows clients to get rid of stacks of papers and get on with being more productive.

15
Drop the Juggling Act
Julie Mahan

What?

A few years ago, I was driving home with my daughters when my cell phone rang. Of course I pride myself on being an excellent multitasker, so I answered my phone. The caller was a co-worker who needed to discuss an important issue. As our conversation progressed, I became immersed in the discussion.

As I cruised along the highway, one of my daughters said, "Mom, where are you going?" I had missed my exit. Not just any exit, but the same exit I have taken every day for the past 10 years. How did I let this happen? I have been a multitasker for years, and this was just one more ball in the air. Right?

Many people say they are great at multitasking because they can juggle several activities at the same time. So, let's take a look at the art of a juggler.

Although they have many things in motion, simultaneously, jugglers are successful because they are only required to touch each thing briefly. It's repetitious – catch and throw, catch and throw. As you get better, you can even begin to add more balls.

Now think about the issues you are dealing with on a day-to-day basis. Even a professional juggler would cringe watching us trying to juggle our problems. We can't just look at a problem for a second and toss it back in the air. We have to look at it, think about it and decide how to act on it. If we juggle too much, we are not allowed the appropriate time to make good choices and act appropriately. The result is little progress and, eventually, all the balls drop.

So What?

Anthony Gatto set a record in 2006 when he juggled eight balls at once for one minute and 13 seconds. That is quite a feat! Compare this world record to our attempts at multitasking. No medal is awarded at the end of 73 seconds. We scurry to keep all the problems in the air, while continuing to introduce additional tasks to our act...all day, every day.

I work in the offices of professionals who have tried the art of multitasking and failed in the long run. They generally have old to-do lists and stacks of paper on their desk, floor and window ledges. Their computers are loaded with a myriad of programs and their shelves are full of unread books...all purchased with the dream that they would be transformed into an efficient, multitasking wizard. Although they try to keep all their tasks in the air...one by one they start to drop. It may not jive with some of the "watercooler advice" we hear in the office, but *multitasking is actually a productivity killer.*

Let's imagine the ultimate multitasker in your office. We will call her Maggie Multitasker. What do we notice about Maggie? She wears a Blackberry on her hip that she frequently pulls out as quickly as a gunfighter in the Old West. Her computer has so many programs running at the same time it is difficult to keep up with everything that is going on. She switches rapidly between running programs, answering pop-up instant messages, and reading new e-mails, all while having a disjointed conversation with a co-worker.

Maggie truly believes that she can and must multitask! If you watch her, you can actually see the juggler in action. Her hands seem to blur as they travel from computer to Blackberry to desk phone to paper. Look into Maggie's eyes and you will see the stress as she eventually drops one or two tasks and loses control.

Does this sound familiar? Do you see Maggie in the mirror? Be honest and admit the truth. There is a rush when we are living on the edge while trying to do it all. Wearing our "Maggie the Multitasker" hat is exciting. We make slow progress on several different projects as we quickly juggle our workload, but we are actually doing a disservice to both our company and ourselves. We get caught in a cycle that prevents us from doing our job well enough to provide opportunities for advancement. That same cycle also prevents us from receiving the satisfaction of a job well done.

While we have the ability and desire to produce excellent work, our constant multitasking typically produces poor results. Switching quickly from one task to another takes too much time. Maggie Multitasker often finds that as soon as she begins making progress on a task, something or someone often distracts her. Then, it takes time to get back into the same frame of mind to continue the previously abandoned task, i.e., unless she is distracted again. The result is often late, poor quality or incomplete work.

Now What?

Multitasking is something that we all do. The Maggie within all of us helps us successfully take on challenges in our profession. What makes a difference is how often, for what length of time and when we multitask. When attempting to do more than one mentally challenging task at the same time, a ball will drop. Remember what happened to me (and probably you, too) while driving and talking on my cell phone. Focusing on the conversation rather than driving caused me to make a simple mistake. It also gave my children the cherished opportunity to roll their eyes at their mother!

How much power does multitasking have during your workday? Do you recognize any of these telltale symptoms?

- Do you have "e-mailitus," which causes you to immediately read all incoming messages?

- Do you answer your Blackberry, pager or cell phone as soon as it goes off?

- Do you find yourself thinking of other tasks during meetings?

- Do you feel like every task must be done now?

If you have reached the point where a constant sense of urgency is consuming your day, you have shifted from being in control to being a juggler. Consider the following ideas to help put some balance back in your day.

Know What's Important. Your best strategy is to stop briefly and re-prioritize your day. This may sound counterintuitive, but if you do not reassess your situation, you will begin dropping the ball. Maybe your day will not turn out as you originally planned, but re-prioritizing will increase your odds of having a successful day.

Slow Down. The Maggie Multitasker within each of us has a blind spot. She confuses being in constant motion with being productive. Are you doing the same? Look over your shoulder into that blind spot. Do you see yourself so busy trying to juggle all of your activities that you are constantly in motion, but rarely accomplishing your goals? It is essential that we examine our activities each day and look for ways to reduce time lost to multitasking.

Show Up. When you plan your work sessions, physically and mentally show up for work. You can invite whomever you want, but you better invite yourself! That statement may sound corny, but the Maggie within will find it a challenge. When you schedule time to do any task, you are the most important participant. One hundred percent of your attention must be there. When an undistracted and uninterrupted "you" is present, you can begin to move mountains.

Focus. Apparently Maggie also has a bit of an ego problem. Maggie often feels indispensable. She makes us feel that we should jump each time our cell phone rings or an e-mail pops up. More than likely, your company is paying you to accomplish a task or project. Results matter more than creating the illusion of indispensability! If your Maggie constantly allows interruptions, she is severely hindering your productivity. Consider these tips:

- Let some calls go to voice mail for an hour.

- Check your e-mails at specific intervals throughout the day.

- Shut your office door for an hour.

- Schedule an alternative workplace, like a conference room, for an hour.

- Schedule protected time on your calendar for working on specific tasks.

The next time you have an opportunity to see a circus, buy a ticket and look for the jugglers. It is truly amazing to watch them in action. It seems like magic when they briefly keep multiple balls, circles, plates or knives in the air. They take their bows and the applause is music to their ears. But for us, there is no easy magic. There are no curtain calls and rarely any applause. However, the show must go on. We must learn to juggle our time wisely with focus and planning, and a few less balls in the air.

"Never confuse motion with action."
– Benjamin Franklin

Sue McGeer
CMS Office Organizers
Modesto, California

209.526.2806
cmsofficeorganizer@sbcglobal.net

During her 26 years in small business and corporate environments as a business owner, manager and administrator, Sue McGeer used her unique ability to create cost-effective office processes and solutions to help colleagues become more organized and improve overall office efficiency.

Experience taught Sue that organized people suffer less stress at work and live more joyful lives, which prompted her to establish her own professional organizing business in order to assist more people. Her services help reduce the high costs associated with disorganization, and include workplace assessments, customized plans, training and coaching.

As a Certified *GO System* Trainer, she teaches business owners, managers and office professionals practical systems for becoming more focused, organized and productive in the workplace.

16
10 "Most Wanted" Productivity Thieves
Sue McGeer

What?

How would you react if someone tipped you off that thieves were breaking into your business or department and stealing your precious resources?

If you are like most of us, you would probably first contact the police and then spring into action to protect against further losses. You might burglarproof your windows and doors or install burglar alarms. Maybe you would hire armed response patrols, security guards or security dogs.

And if someone tipped you off that thousands of dollars worth of profits were quietly disappearing inside your business, you might call in a loss prevention expert or a private detective to conduct an investigation, find the culprits and take corrective action.

Certainly, no reasonable person knowingly stands by while they are being robbed, and everyone would agree that the price of security is money well invested.

So What?

Here's a tip-off: Productivity thieves (PTs) are at work inside most businesses. They steal hundreds of hours a year and thousands of dollars from the bottom line of unsuspecting business owners.

Ten "Most Wanted" PTs have been identified through numerous reports, surveys and studies. Their identities and descriptions are posted here so business owners and employees can be on the lookout for them, expose them, and end their potential to steal profits. Encountering just a few of these culprits can steal the better part of your time and energy on any given day.

Caution: These PTs are dangerous to the health of your business. If any are operating in your business, they are costing you a significant amount of money and creating serious problems. Let's make some assumptions* and estimate what these PTs might be costing. (PT estimates are based on a salary of $48,000 and a 240-day working year.)

1. **Lack of organizing skills.** Many white-collar workers and managers waste 40 percent to 90 percent of their workday because they have never been taught organizing skills to help them cope with their increasing workloads. For example, most businesses provide employees with e-mail capabilities, but never teach them how to use e-mail properly. As a result, employees use e-mail ineffectively and waste time on unproductive activities.

    Productivity loss estimate (65 percent as an average):

Daily	Annually	Cost per person
312 mins	1248 hrs/31.2 wks	$31,200

2. **Interruptions.** During a typical day, interruptions due to communication technology use (phones, e-mails, PDAs, etc.) and unproductive co-worker interactions occur about every eight minutes. Although the average interruption lasts about five minutes, the actual loss in productivity can sometimes be twice the duration of the interruption due to the loss of focused attention and the lost time associated with switching between tasks. When returning to their original task, workers often repeat previously performed activities in an effort to retrace what they were doing before the interruption. Assuming only three five-minute interruptions per hour, and the resulting "doubling effect" on the productivity loss due to switching tasks and repeating activities, a worker can easily waste half their workday dealing with interruptions.

   Productivity loss estimate:

Daily	Annually	Cost per person
240 mins	960 hrs/24 wks	$24,000

3. **Information retrieval.** Time spent searching for nonexistent information, failing to find existing information, or recreating information that can't be found, steals from 15 percent to 50 percent of workers' time.

   Productivity loss estimate (32.5 percent as an average):

Daily	Annually	Cost per person
156 mins	624 hrs/15.6 wks	$15,600

4. **Meetings.** Meetings that start late, run overtime, include lengthy debates and off-agenda discussions, steal about an hour-and-a-half of productive time per day for executives.

Productivity loss estimate:

Daily	Annually	Cost per person
90 mins	360 hrs/9 wks	$9,000

5. **Multitasking.** Simultaneously trying to do several things at once results in productivity losses of 20 to 40 percent.

    Productivity loss estimate (30 percent decrease in productivity and estimating four hours per day multitasking):

Daily	Annually	Cost per person
72 mins	288 hrs/7.2 wks	$7,200

6. **Paper handling.** Executives waste about 240 hours per year and nonexecutive employees waste about 400 hours per year searching for documents.

    Productivity loss estimate (320 hours as an average):

Daily	Annually	Cost per person
80 mins	320 hrs/8 wks	$8,000

7. **Communication.** Poor communication steals about 320 hours per year. Medical costs and other expenditures caused by conflict with colleagues, loss of job satisfaction, and strained personal relationships, add to the loss.

    Productivity loss estimate:

Daily	Annually	Cost per person
80 mins	320 hrs/8 wks	$8,000

8. **Phone calls.** Conversations take an average of five minutes longer when they lack direction, or when failure to obtain appropriate information on the initial call requires a follow-up call. Workers average 52 phone calls a day.

Productivity loss estimate (average of 12 poorly planned calls each day):

Daily	Annually	Cost per person
60 mins	240 hrs/6 wks	$6,000

9. **Trips away from the desk.** Trips to the fax machine, copier, printer, co-workers' desks, restroom and break room take workers away from their desks an average of 80 times per week. Interruptions and hallway meetings along the way increase the average length of a trip.

Productivity loss estimate (16 as a daily average; two-minute direct trips):

Daily	Annually	Cost per person
32 mins	28 hrs/3.2 wks	$3,200

Productivity loss estimate (five-minute interruptions on 25 percent of the above trips):

Daily	Annually	Cost per person
20 mins	80 hrs/2 wks	$2,000

10. **Waiting.** The cost of a minute for someone earning a salary of $48,000 is about $0.42. If three people spend five minutes waiting for a meeting to begin, the $2.10 cost per person seems negligible, but the impact of the group productivity loss quickly adds up over time!

Productivity loss estimate (five-minute waiting period occurs twice a day):

Daily	Annually	Cost per person
10 mins	40 hrs/1 wk	$1,000

Now What?

You can make your own assumptions and play around with the numbers. The point is, PTs can and are probably costing you a lot of money. Take action to protect your business and employees from these PTs. Training to improve employee organizing skills and increase their productivity typically costs a fraction of most of the potential losses listed previously.

Begin with these protective steps:

1. **Organizing skills.** Hire a professional organizer who can accurately assess your potential for productivity improvements and provide training to help your employees become more focused, organized and productive.

2. **Interruptions.** Add up to 30 productive minutes to a working hour by turning off communication technology for that hour.

3. **Information.** Use search engine tools and efficient processes for storage and recovery of information.

4. **Meetings.** Allocate time limits for agenda items and monitor them with a timer to maintain focus and prevent rambling discussions. Note off-agenda topics and, if necessary, address them later. Stay on topic!

5. **Multitasking.** Focus on one task at a time. Give the task at hand your full attention. Get closure on the task and then move on to the next task and give it your full attention.

6. **Paper handling.** Eliminate paper searches by using a document classifying and processing system that allows you to find things when you need them and keep your office free of clutter.

7. **Communication.** Avoid time-consuming confusion. When in doubt, immediately clarify instructions or expectations.

8. **Phone calls.** Before making a call, draft a brief agenda to guide the conversation and help accomplish your goals.

9. **Trips away from your desk.** Minimize trips away from your desk, especially when you are in the middle of an important task. When making a necessary trip away from your desk, minimize unnecessary distractions.

10. **Waiting.** If possible, use waiting time productively. For example, carry a casual reading file to appointments and meetings and use any waiting time to read and think. Also consider using waiting time to simply relax, refocus and replenish your energy.

Maybe PTs are costing you less than these estimates; maybe they are costing more. Remember, these estimates are based on the cost *per person*. Imagine what productivity losses are costing large organizations when you consider all employees. The good news is that it doesn't take superheroes or master crime fighters to minimize or eliminate these PTs. It just takes a little common sense and a commitment to making small, incremental improvements. Just as the costs add up quickly when you ignore these issues, the benefits add up just as quickly when you take the time and effort to take corrective action. Arrest the progress of the 10 "Most Wanted" in your organization and watch your bottom line grow.

---

* For more information on the sources used to identify these PTs and the estimated productivity losses, please contact the author directly.

Beverly Miller
Your Organizing Coach
Auburn, Washington

253.737.LIFE
Beverly@yourorganizingcoach.com
www.yourorganizingcoach.com

Beverly Miller lives near the city of Seattle in the beautiful Pacific Northwest state of Washington. She considers it a blessing that her two sons and three grandsons live in the same community. Not only a "born organizer," Beverly is also an avid music lover and has taken up her childhood instrument once again – the harp!

Beverly developed and refined her organizing skills during her 25 years in the retail business. In 2004, through her exceptional management of 30 staff members, the Christian Booksellers Association (CBA) awarded her location with the coveted National Store of the Year. Beverly is a past presenter at both national and regional CBA conventions, a member of the National Association of Professional Organizers (NAPO), and is a qualified *Paper Tiger* and *GO System* consultant.

Beverly's life mission is to inspire others to make positive life changes by creating beauty and order. Through her encouragement, organizational aptitude and ability to streamline multi-dimensional processes, she enhances productivity in her clients' homes and businesses.

17
So, What's Stopping You?
Beverly Miller

What?

I was tired…aching…cold and had just awakened about one hour into my red-eye flight to Boston. With at least four hours remaining before landing, I decided to ask the flight attendant for a blanket. It was a reasonable request, but something was stopping me from asking. In order to understand my reluctance, you need to understand that I rarely feel comfortable "bothering" others with such requests. After all, the flight attendant might consider me annoying or might be too busy doing more important things. I rationalized that my request could disturb others around me and thought I might be perceived as too demanding or needy.

Looking around, I noticed a number of passengers with blankets, so this was certainly not an inappropriate request. Thoughts about my request marched around my mind…they seemed to be searching for some risk-free way to escape and be heard. Should I have asked sooner? This far into the flight, the majority of the passengers were sleeping soundly and the flight attendant might not be able to find a blanket anyway. If I had only brought along a coat, I mused, then I wouldn't be in this situation.

I considered getting up and quietly asking the attendant, but I was in a window seat and pretty much trapped. What would my seatmates think if I asked them to let me out? After considering my options, I pulled my sweater tightly around me, sat up straight and glanced at the little call button above my head. It was only about 18 inches away, but I still hesitated. For some reason, I was clearly uncomfortable making a simple request for a blanket. I somehow pushed through my anxiety and reached up to press the button. As I *raised my hand* and pressed the button, a distant but specific childhood memory flashed through my mind. Suddenly, a stream of thoughts about this childhood experience flooded my mind.

It was years earlier and I was a little girl in school. I don't remember much else about that particular day, however, I'll never forget when the teacher asked a question and no one else seemed to know the answer. It was my first day in a new school and a new state...I didn't know anyone. However, I knew the answer to the teacher's question, so I confidently *raised my hand*. The teacher called on me and I proudly gave the answer, "Ten." "What?" she responded, as if she couldn't hear, and then asked me to repeat my answer. This went on a few times until she finally asked me to write my answer on the chalkboard. I was terrified! Was my answer wrong? Did I miss some hidden, "tricky" part of the question? Uh oh...why did I raise my hand? My thoughts started racing wildly and I questioned everything I knew to be true. When I wrote the number "10" on the board, she exclaimed, "Oh! Why didn't you say *ten*?"

Having just moved from Illinois to Alaska, my teacher was apparently confused by my accent. For what seemed an eternity, I stood in front of the class while she slowly pronounced the word "ten" and asked me to repeat it. Since I apparently made little progress after several attempts, she informed me that I would have to stay after school until I learned to properly pronounce the word "ten." I felt totally humiliated! I learned a lesson that day. I didn't learn how to properly pronounce the word "ten," however, for the rest of that year, throughout junior high and high school…I learned to *never raise my hand* in class again.

Suddenly the flight attendant disrupted my trip down memory lane and asked me what I needed. His tone was neither helpful nor negative, just matter-of-fact. Yet, somehow, sitting there and having just *raised my hand*, I felt like a child again. I quietly and respectfully voiced my request for a blanket, and after a cursory look around my seat; he responded with, "I'll see if I can find one for you." He never returned. The lesson I learned many years before was once again reinforced. I should *never raise my hand*.

So What?

What was going on? I did nothing wrong or inappropriate. I knew that most people would be quite comfortable making such a simple request. Yet, I had hesitated and felt quite uncomfortable. As I reflected on my situation, I began to realize that my mind was replaying some old familiar tapes; I didn't want to call attention to myself, I didn't want to be an annoyance, I didn't want to interrupt anyone. The circumstances had somehow activated some of my traumatic childhood memories. Some people refer to these childhood memories and their associated feelings as tapes, since they operate somewhat like tape recordings. These mental tapes created long ago are easily activated and replayed when you experience current events that remind you of the circumstances that created the original memories. Sights, smells, sounds and other sensory experiences or events can activate the tapes. Interestingly, although we may have chronologically reached adulthood, certain circumstances can trigger a childhood experience causing us to respond physically and emotionally like a child. Reluctance to ask for a blanket on an airplane is certainly not a significant or life-limiting issue. However, the same sort of psychological issues that made my blanket request difficult can prevent people from asking for business, a well-earned raise, a promotion or various forms of help or assistance. Childhood tapes can stop adulthood progress!

Everyone carries many childhood tapes with them into their adult life. Some tapes are joyful and aid us well in life. Most of us who had responsible parents have the "look both ways before you cross the street" tape. This tape served us well as children and continues to serve us well as adults. However, some of these tapes can severely inhibit or stop our progress in life. Here are some typical self-defeating or inhibiting tapes that many of us might be familiar with:

"Quit asking for so much all the time."

"Can't you do anything right?"

"Stop whining all the time, nobody likes a complainer."

"Mind your own business."

"You'll never amount to anything."

"Put that back, we can't afford it."

"Why are you always bothering everyone?"

"You were our *surprise* child."

Think about the real message behind some of these comments or how a child might interpret them. Many of these tapes can resurface in our adult lives and create minor inconveniences or major problems. If any of these tapes are familiar to you or if they trigger similar tapes, then read on.

Now What?

One of the best ways to deal with tapes is to literally overwrite them. How? Start by *becoming more aware of the times when a tape seems to be influencing your behavior*. Look for signs that indicate your behavior is not in alignment with your true desires. For example, anytime you say "yes" when you really want to say "no," or you say "no" when you really want to say "yes," or you find yourself not asking for what you really want, or you feel very uncomfortable expressing your true feelings, there is a good chance that a tape is influencing your behavior. *By becoming aware of these tapes, you can begin the process of challenging and revising them!* As an adult, when your inner voices say things like "stop asking for so much," mentally challenge your thinking and ask yourself, "Is this request reasonable given the circumstances? Would a reasonable and rational adult have any problem asking for this?"

Revisiting our encounter with the intimidating flight attendant and his call button, rather than wondering why some mysterious force is preventing you from pushing the button and asking for a blanket, you could logically assume that one of those tapes must be keeping you from asking for what you want. I'll bet it has to do with everyone around me being too busy to hear my request and the sense of being an annoyance when asking for something as a child. Asking for a blanket is no big deal. I want a blanket; it's a reasonable request...so I will ask for it. All they can do is say no. Again, the blanket request dilemma is a minor life issue. You can probably work out such tapes on your own. However, imagine the tapes that can be created by abusive parents or caretakers, alcoholic parents, major childhood traumas such as the early death of a parent or sibling, a house fire, an embarrassing experience, etc. You may need to consider working with a professional counselor to deal with some of the more serious life tapes.

What has all this got to do with your productivity? As your life unfolds, some tapes can negatively impact your ability to perform your job duties and can seriously inhibit or stop your career progress. Take the time to look for signs in your life where your behavior is not in alignment with your true desires. What are you saying "no" or "yes" to in life when you really want to say the opposite? Are you asking for what you really want out of life? Are you struggling with some counter-productive childhood tapes that need to be overwritten? *So, what's stopping you?*

Carla Miller
This Way Up
Dallas, Texas

817.296.7507
carla@thiswayupcoach.com
www.thiswayupcoach.com

As founder and president of This Way Up, Carla Miller is passionate about helping people grow. She uses her talents as a teacher, coach and speaker to help people become more productive and efficient in their lives. Carla loves watching people light up as they experience those "aha" moments that truly change the way they work and, ultimately, live.

Carla is a Certified *GO System* Trainer, speaker, ordained minister and life coach. She is also the author of the book *Ready or Not for the Emergencies of Life*. Carla is a member of both the National Association of Professional Organizers (NAPO) and the Network for Productivity Excellence (NPEX). She also offers workshops on "Creating Your Best Life" which helps people to decide what they want out of life, create their personal road map to success, and take action toward creating that life.

When Carla is not working with others, she enjoys having fun with friends, reading, watching movies and traveling.

18
You Must Be Present and Participate
Carla Miller

What?

In the spring of 1967, bicycles with banana seats were the rage among kids my age. These bikes had baskets with neon-colored plastic flowers around the edge, colorful streamers coming out of the handlebars and, if you were truly lucky, a bell! I really wanted a bicycle with a banana seat. I loved to ride and a bike would give me more of the freedom I craved to ride to my friends' houses.

As luck or fate would have it, the elementary school principal announced that the Quaker Oats Company was promoting a physical fitness event at the junior high school. All elementary schoolkids were *invited to participate*. The teachers explained that we would be judged on our ability to do sit-ups, pull-ups, run, etc., and we would get a certificate at the end of the day. Even more exciting was the fact that the local Jaycees were sponsoring the event and giving away a *purple bicycle with a banana seat*. The moment I heard about the giveaway, I knew the bicycle was mine! All week long, I told my parents over and over that I was going to win that bicycle. Their warnings that many other boys and girls would be there trying to win the bicycle fell on deaf ears. I knew without a shadow of a doubt the bicycle was mine!

The day of the event, I woke up early thinking about *my* bicycle. I ran all the way to the school. We completed the physical fitness events at noon and gathered on the tennis courts. All the children lined up behind the nets. I was at the very front of the group, so excited I couldn't stand it! The sponsors shouted, "Who's going to win the bicycle?" As I jumped up and down waving my arms in the air, I screamed back, "I am!" The next thing I knew, they announced, "…and the winner is…Carla Miller." *My* bike would be delivered to my house that afternoon.

I ran home and shouted, "I won the bike!" Needless to say, my parents were a bit surprised by the news. That afternoon, two men arrived with my new purple bike with a banana seat. I sat on the bike while someone took my picture for the newspaper. Later, my dad added a basket with neon flowers, colorful streamers, and – of course – a bell! It was the perfect bike and one of the best days of my life!

So What?

In order to get the purple bike, I had to be present and I had to participate. As an adult, my life goals no longer include purple bikes, or bicycle streamers, or bicycle bells. I have outgrown the bike…but I haven't outgrown the lesson I learned when I got that bike. In life, you must be present and participate to get what you want.

So what do you want out of life? What do you want to do, be or have?

The process of being *present* means you cannot allow regrets, past failures, doubts, etc., to rob you of the joy of living in the present. As a little girl, I didn't know any better. I took mental ownership of the bike several days before I took physical ownership. I experienced joyful feelings in the present moment...every moment...from the time I decided to get the bike until I took physical possession of it. And part of the process of *participating* means you must be clear about your intentions and focused on what you want. Children and older people seem to be great at knowing what they really want in life. Lack of clarity seems to primarily exist between these two age groups. That's another lesson for another day, but you might want to think about why that occurs, if it is happening to you. For now, be clear about what you want.

There is a lot of talk these days about something called The Law of Attraction. In a nutshell, The Law of Attraction states that you attract things and experiences in your life with your thoughts, feelings and actions. For example, like-minded people tend to attract each other and you attract experiences that you think about often. Happy people attract happy people and happy experiences. Happy people don't want to be around complainers. Complainers, on the other hand, often feel comfortable around other complainers and the very situation they are complaining about. Gripe about the poor service at a restaurant and you are likely to get more of it. Simply stated, like attracts like. What we focus on is what we tend to get in life...good or bad. I still can't totally explain it...but I am convinced my joyful and unabashed focus on that purple bike had much to do with me getting it.

Now What?

Consider the various aspects of your life. For example, your family life, career, finances, health, relationships, leisure time, spiritual life, you get the idea. Here are some simple tips that can help you get what you want.

Step 1: Clarify Your Intention

Decide what you want in each of these areas. What do you want to do, be or have? Let's use your career goals as an example. When you consider your career, do you want to work less, work more, earn more, be more productive or be more organized? Once you decide what you want, write down your goals and describe *in detail* all you want to be, do and have in your career.

Step 2: Visualize

Now that you have written down your goals and described in detail all you want to be, do and have, sit back, relax, close your eyes and visualize everything you described.

You might also consider making a collage of your life. For example, if you want to start leaving work in time to be home for dinner with your family, put a picture of you and your family around the dinner table on your collage. Imagine how it feels to be so productive at work that you are able to relax at home in the evening with your family.

Step 3: Have Faith...Believe in Your Vision

Having faith gives power to your thoughts. Norman Vincent Peale said, *"If you keep your eyes open expectantly every day for great and wonderful things to happen, it is astonishing that great and wonderful things will tend to happen to you. Always think the best. What you think habitually will tend to happen. What we send out mentally and spiritually will return to us."* He goes on to explain that we should expect a miracle, *"not as a strange happening unknown to scientific procedures, but as a great and wonderful quality that can be brought to pass."* We have to have faith. Have faith in your Creator, believe that you deserve the best, and be willing to accept and enjoy good things that happen in your life.

Step 4: Feel It

Get excited about your vision! Your emotions are one of your best, and possibly only, sources of direct knowledge. Your emotions tell you when and if you are on the right track in life. When you experience negative emotions, it often means you are focused on what you *do not want* to happen. Don't deny or try to ignore negative emotions; use them to help initiate the process of reframing your thinking. It is usually a simple matter to pivot your thinking and begin focusing on what you *do want* to happen.

Step 5: Be Grateful

Be grateful for the good things in your life. Although it may seem as if everything is going wrong at times, it is always possible to find something good about your life. If you don't believe it, read *Man's Search for Meaning* by Viktor Frankl. It is a powerful book about choosing to maintain a healthy attitude even under the direst of circumstances. Be grateful for what you have and where you are today, and begin to build a new life on your current blessings. If this is something new for you,

you might try taking a few moments to write down what you are grateful for at the beginning of each day.

Step 6: Take Action

Martin Luther King, Jr. said, *"Take the first step in faith. You don't have to see the whole staircase, just take the first step."* You don't always have to know everything you will have to do or exactly how everything will unfold before you begin. You just need to take the next best step you can think of that will begin to move you in the right direction. In this sense, taking the next step is about relaxing and following your instincts more than forcing things. Ask almost anyone who has built a successful business, made a great discovery, or otherwise accomplished great things in life. If they are honest, they will tell you their initial plans went through many changes and adaptations as things unfolded.

All the preceding steps will serve to help you show up in the present and participate in your own life. As a little girl, I didn't know any better than to simply decide that I wanted a purple bike and to show up at the appointed time and participate in the process that allowed me to get it. What are the "purple bikes" in your life that you want, but are not getting? What are you doing to make sure you are both present and participating to receive these "purple bikes" as they show up in your life?

Nicole Pittaluga, MA
The Productive Professional, LLC
Chatham, New Jersey

973.479.9778
nicole@p4productivity.com
www.p4productivity.com

For many, staying motivated and on track is a daily struggle. Life has so many demands it can sometimes be overwhelming. Nicole understands these challenges, has learned how to master the juggling act, and now greatly enjoys helping her clients do the same!

An eternal optimist, Nicole believes that every problem can be solved with a concerted work ethic and a fresh perspective. She helps individuals in midsize to large corporations identify their true life's purpose, unlock their ability to reach it, and lead the professional and personal lives they want to live – not have to live.

Nicole is a Certified *GO System* Trainer and a *Paper Tiger* Authorized Consultant (PTAC). She is an active member of the National Association of Professional Organizers (NAPO) and serves as secretary for the Northern New Jersey Chapter.

19
Calmer Waters
Nicole Pittaluga

What?

As a child, I feared the ocean. On hot summer days at the beach, I wanted to splash around with my brother in the calm area just a short distance from the shoreline. Yet, the ocean was so big and powerful, the thought of going out that far overwhelmed me. I struggled to make it past the spot where waves crashed on the shore. Visions of scenes from the movies *Jaws* and *Piranha II* stopped me in the water at knee level as I wondered about frightful creatures lurking beneath the surface.

Every time I mustered the courage to go deeper, out near my brother in the calm area, my mother's warning to be careful and watch out for the undertow further reinforced my fears. I knew she was right...because I was once caught in the undertow. I hated being swirled around, getting water up my nose, not knowing what to do. I panicked and tried to catch my breath and regain my footing before the next wave crashed on top of me. Tiny rocks, broken seashells and swirling sand scratched my skin. An adult finally grabbed me and pulled me from the path of an oncoming wave. I was terrified!

Sometimes, when distraught clients describe the challenges they face at work, I am reminded of my childhood experiences with the ocean. Like the ocean, the scope of their responsibility can be massive, with daunting forces at play and many unknown issues lurking about beneath the surface of things. In this situation, it's easy to see how they lose sight of their priorities. Their various roles and responsibilities in life compete for their limited time and attention. These people often feel as if they are caught in the undertow of whirling activities, swirling around, wondering what to do...trying to catch their breath...seeking calmer waters.

So What?

You may leave your office at the end of a long day wondering where the time went and what you accomplished. You may vow that tomorrow will be different...but when the next day rolls around, you are once again overwhelmed before you can regain your footing. Keep this up long enough and you start to feel burned out and hopeless.

One common productivity killer often creates this vicious and overwhelming cycle. Consider the demands on your time and energy during a typical day. As e-mails, voice mails, paper and verbal requests pile up, *it's easy to get in the habit of ignoring your priorities and responding to the demands of others.* At first it feels great (and productive) when you delete an e-mail, return a call or shuffle a few papers. Unfortunately, when you realize that the end of the day or month is rapidly approaching, and *your* project is due...and you are nowhere near finished...you also realize you have a big problem!

It's simple. When the majority of your day is spent responding to the priorities of others, you are not likely to get your own work done. It feels as if everyone is constantly taking bites of your time and energy…like little piranhas lurking under the surface of the ocean.

Now What?

If you find yourself constantly responding to the demands of others and ignoring your own priorities, it's time to get out of the swirling waves and into the calmer water before you experience serious consequences. There are some key differences between extremely productive workers, swimming in the calm waters, and those stuck in the undertow of the work world.

Extremely productive workers are proactive, not reactive.

First, redefine your priorities. Instead of using your limited energy on other people's priorities, whenever possible, use your energy to do your own work first. Clarify your responsibilities and define the desired outcomes for your projects. Clearly define the steps for each project, the person responsible for each step and the timeline for completion of each step.

Make sure your projects stay on track by scheduling appointments with yourself and considering these appointments as important as an appointment with your best client. Shut your door, put your phone on "do not disturb," close down your e-mail program and get to work. Stay focused on your project until you get closure on what you decided to accomplish.

Extremely productive people know when to say "no."

When faced with a demand for your attention, ask yourself:

- How does this request relate to my own projects and priorities?

- Is it my responsibility?

- How does this request stack up against my priorities in terms of my team's overall goals? Is it more important, less important or equally important?

- What are the potential consequences of saying "no"?

Extremely productive people are masters of delegation.

It is important to recognize when it is best to delegate work, even if it takes longer. You may have the knowledge and experience to solve the problem, however, consider how you acquired this knowledge and experience. Chances are, you learned by working through a similar situation yourself. Delegating work helps others learn and grow, and frees up your time for more important tasks. Offer guidance, but assign responsibility where it belongs.

Extremely productive people are good at setting boundaries.

Know exactly what you are agreeing to do. Clarify expectations and deadlines. Someone else's crisis does not have to become your emergency. Let others know when their expectations are unrealistic. As you make the transition to this proactive approach, you will have to retrain others to be considerate of your time and to ask for help in advance. Remember, if you supervise others, you serve as the role model for the entire team. If you operate in crisis mode, your team will too.

Let people know your preferred method of receiving requests. Limit the number of times per day you check your e-mail, voice mail and in-box. If you feel it is necessary, set up an auto-reply e-mail message informing recipients that you will only check and respond to incoming messages a few times daily. If people truly need you immediately, they can usually find a way to contact you.

Extremely productive people do work that utilizes their natural talents.

Helping others at the expense of your own priorities may be an avoidance strategy or a form of procrastination in disguise. Two common reasons for such procrastination are boredom and anxiety about moving out of your comfort zone. When you are bored at work, helping someone can provide relief, especially if they are asking you to do something that you find easy to do. At the other extreme, if the task is new and uncomfortable, your natural response may be avoidance. In these situations, it is important to recognize the nature of the challenge. No one can be good at everything. Is the challenge stretching your current natural abilities or is it requiring you to perform tasks that are not in alignment with your natural strengths? For example, some people are very introverted and more task-oriented than people-oriented. It is rarely a good idea to put these people in a position where they must constantly interact with others. It would be better to find a naturally extroverted person to handle such a task.

Surprisingly, mismatches between an employee's natural strengths and the job they are asked to perform are quite common in many organizations. If the majority of your responsibilities do not energize you and utilize your natural talents and skills, your work may be a poor fit for you. Consider renegotiating your responsibilities and structuring your work in a way that capitalizes on your unique talents.

Look for specific skills to address any problems related to challenging situations.

In general, there are two ways to "calm the waters" and deal with any fears or anxieties related to challenging situations. You can increase your skill level related to specific challenges or *decrease the challenges*. The first option – increasing your skills – is typically thought of as the best (and sometimes only) strategy. After all, who is willing to admit that they can't handle a challenge? I'll tell you who is willing to admit such a thing. Smart people! It is OK to admit you are getting in over your head. It is OK to admit you need help. It is OK to set boundaries. It is OK to say "no" at times. If you feel the undertow of a challenge is pulling you down, identify the specific skill or skills that are needed to meet the challenge and ask for help. Find people who have mastered the required skills and learn as much as you can from them. In the end, do not accept a challenge that is beyond your current capabilities without making it clear that you might need some help. Smart people know when they are getting in over their heads and know when to ask for help.

Many people seem to be resigned to the fact that their lives, especially their work lives, are always going to be turbulent. They have become habituated to a daily life of struggles, extreme challenges and crisis management. They are simply wrong! Yes, you should expect occasional turbulence...but it should not be a continuous way of life. Try some of these ideas and see if you can find more ways to create calmness in your life. Work your way through the waves crashing onto the shore and spend more of your life out in the calmer waters.

Stephanie Pyle, MBA
Organizing by Design
 – Abundant Productivity
Cheyenne, Wyoming

307.634.4765
sapyle@msn.com
www.abundantproductivity.com

Increased productivity should not feel like an unattainable goal. Stephanie Pyle, owner of Organizing by Design – Abundant Productivity, understands the struggles facing busy professionals today. She started her business in 2005 and now consults with professionals from all industries to help them increase productivity and organization to more easily reach their goals. She loves the challenge of designing customized solutions and working with individuals who are ready to make a difference in their lives by embracing life-changing habits.

In addition to working with individuals, Stephanie also provides customized training for organizations of all sizes. She is a frequent presenter on various topics related to productivity and organizing. Whether individually or in a group setting, Stephanie's passion for productivity and organizing is evident. She is a member of the National Association of Professional Organizers (NAPO) and the Greater Cheyenne Chamber of Commerce.

20
Conquering Productivity Traps
Stephanie Pyle

What?

The organizing industry is full of veteran organizers and productivity consultants with a wealth of knowledge to share. I benefit immensely from their collective wisdom. However, I have found that sometimes the greatest lessons in life come from my children.

As any veteran parent knows, when peaceful, serene quietness is in the air, mayhem and mischief are undoubtedly brewing. Such was the case one summer day in 2006. My six-year-old son had recently purchased a lasso in his quest to become a cowboy. As I approached his room to get to the bottom of the uncanny quiet lingering over our home, I saw a look of great pride on my son's face. What I saw behind him was startling and humorous at the same time. He had woven his lasso back-and-forth from one side of his room to the other in a spiderweb fashion. When I asked him about this tangled weave, he proudly told me that he had created a trap for his two-year-old sister. As I fought back the laughter and expressed the dangers of setting traps for others, I thought about how this "trap setting" provided valuable insight into the world of productivity.

I realized that as busy professionals, we sometimes set traps for ourselves. How do we do this? We overcommit ourselves, take on more than we can realistically handle and find ourselves rushing at every turn. In essence, we set productivity traps that undermine our goals and rob us of valuable opportunities for success.

So What?

When we set productivity traps for ourselves, we are successful at one thing. We create chaos for ourselves by building an environment that makes it nearly impossible to function. This creates a myriad of negative feelings and consequences. When we operate in the midst of such chaos, we often feel frustrated, anxious, imbalanced and disappointed – with others and ourselves. Unfortunately, this prevents us from reaching our goals and living fulfilling lives. I work with many professionals who struggle with these issues. My biggest challenge, however, has not been any particular client. Rather, my biggest challenge has been taming the chaos and imbalance in my own life. Over the years, I frequently held down a full-time job, kept volunteer commitments, furthered my education, and occasionally took on additional jobs just for the experience, all while raising a growing family. Looking back, it seems like a blur. That, however, pales in comparison to the chapter in my life when I started my own business. At that point, the speed of everything seemed to increase by 50 percent.

As I became busier and the chaos threatened to grow to unmanageable proportions, I decided it was time for a different approach. I was tired of setting productivity traps for myself. Many of my clients unknowingly set productivity traps too. I reached the conclusion that life is too short to continue operating in such an energy-draining manner. Productivity traps must stop if we are to reach our highest personal and professional potential.

Now What?

This realization led to manageable resolutions using the 80/20 principle. The 80/20 principle is a powerful phenomenon that we can observe in every aspect of our lives. This principle holds that 80 percent of our results come from 20 percent of our efforts. When we apply the 80/20 principle to our lives, we can achieve extremely powerful results.

We must do three things to stop productivity traps from inhibiting our success. First, we must evaluate our business and personal activities and determine if they are meaningful to our lives. Second, we need to adjust our attitudes toward our responsibilities and commitments. Finally, we need to apply the 80/20 principle to our daily activities.

Step 1. Evaluate your business and personal activities and determine if they are meaningful to your life.

Given the responsibilities and commitments of most busy professionals today, they rarely take time for evaluation and reflection. However, reflection about the past can hold valuable insights for the future. I embraced the concept of reflection when I read *The 80/20 Principle* by Richard Koch. In this book, there is a meaningful exercise that puts activities and commitments into perspective. This is a modified version of the exercise.

Write the following headings on four separate sheets of paper:

List 1: Activities that create happiness (energy builders)

List 2: Great achievements and moves in the right direction

List 3: Activities that create unhappiness (energy drains)

List 4: Achievement thieves and moves in the wrong direction

Once you have each heading on a piece of paper, reflect on and write down activities that fall into the appropriate categories. Include both personal and professional aspects of your life. In doing this exercise, I reviewed my calendar for a period of six months. The activities or commitments that conjured up positive, successful feelings went on list 1 or 2. The activities or commitments that conjured up negative emotions went on list 3 or 4. When I completed the exercise, I considered the activities on lists 3 and 4 that were still a part of my life. Those activities were sent to the chopping block. By eliminating, greatly reducing or modifying these activities, I was able to turn my time and energy away from activities that were not adding value to my life. This put me in a position to use this valuable time and energy for more activities on lists 1 and 2. This exercise was a process; it did not happen overnight. When going through this exercise you will likely realize, as I did, that 80 percent of our enjoyment and success comes from 20 percent of our activities and achievements.

Step 2. Adjust your attitudes toward responsibilities and commitments.

What does attitude have to do with attaining goals? When we constantly feel overwhelmed, overloaded, stressed and anxious, these feelings dominate our lives and become our reality.

Try embracing feelings of natural productivity, freedom from strife, success, optimism and effective composure. When you are satisfied that you are focused on the proper responsibilities and commitments for this season of your life, approach them with a positive, optimistic and even thankful attitude. If you struggle with this from time to time, seek comfort in prayer, meditation or guidance from a close friend or advisor who can help you discern if you are on the right track. Develop a positive approach and know you accepted these responsibilities and commitments for a good reason. Feel optimistic that you can and will successfully accomplish the challenges presented by your responsibilities. Maintain a thankful attitude that you are afforded such an incredible opportunity to be successful each and every day. Spend 20 percent of your day deliberately adopting a positive attitude. This will undoubtedly impact the other 80 percent of your life.

Step 3. Apply the 80/20 principle to your daily activities.

Conventional wisdom tells us that we do not really suffer from a shortage of time; the real problem is how we use our time. At the beginning of each week, consider your most important goals. Then, block off 20 percent of your time each day to focus on activities that move you closer to your goals. You do not have to fully achieve the goal on a particular day; simply do something that moves you closer to the goal than you were the day before. If this sounds unrealistic, consider the fact that 20 percent of an eight-hour workday is only 96 minutes. Do you have 96 minutes a day to make a vast difference in your own life?

If you feel you do not have an extra five minutes per day, much less 96 minutes, then it is time to ask yourself some serious questions. Are you bogged down on busy work that does not truly lead to the results you want? Do you have trouble delegating work to others? Are you saying "yes" when you should be saying "no"? The longer you do things the same way, the more difficult it is to change your habits when necessary. However, that is not a good reason to keep the same habits forever. Consider how liberating it would be to let go of the routine activities that do not add value to your day. Consider your activities next week, and for each major task ask yourself why you are doing it. Explore ways to apply the 80/20 principle and achieve more powerful results than you ever imagined. Ask a trusted friend to help you keep your 80/20 commitments.

Productivity traps have no place in a successful person's life. When you feel chaos approaching, consider three simple words: evaluate, adjust and apply. Evaluate your commitments, adjust your attitude and apply the 80/20 principle. Remember, becoming more productive is not a destination to be reached...it is an ongoing process of growth, learning and opportunity.

Cheryl Robertson
Defining Spaces
Newburyport, Massachusetts

978.314.2583
DefiningSpaces@verizon.net
www.DefiningSpacesUSA.com

Cheryl Robertson is passionate about helping others become more organized and efficient so they have the time to do the things they love to do.

Cheryl has over 25 years of experience working for private corporations and municipal governments in the field of accounting and finance. Her roles as accounting manager, controller and finance director provide a broad range of experience in managing, budgeting, time management and computerization. She brings this experience to Defining Spaces, which she founded in 2006.

Cheryl teaches her clients office organizing, time management skills and stress management techniques to give them a more satisfied feeling of being productive, focused and stress-free in their workplace.

21
What Message Does Your Office Send?
Cheryl Robertson

What?

How do you feel when you walk into your office? Do you feel energetic, uplifted and ready for a highly productive day? Does everything in your office have a place? Is everything in its place? Do you have a system for handling your incoming correspondence, e-mails, voice mails, etc.? At the end of your day, is everything neatly put away? Is your desktop reasonably clear? Is your work prioritized for the beginning of the next day? How do others feel when they walk into your office?

There is a bit of a debate going on now among people who write books and articles on organization regarding the merits or drawbacks of working in a messy office. If you like your messy office and it somehow enhances your productivity as some writers indicate...stick with what is working for you. However, keep in mind that just because you like your mess, that doesn't mean everyone, including your boss and clients, feel the same way. All else being equal, people generally prefer to put their trust in those who appear to have some measure of control over their life and workload.

Your office certainly does not have to be pristine. After all, it is a place to work and ...it is OK to be messy at times. However, if you don't have well-defined systems and processes for keeping reasonable order in your office, you probably use one of three methods to cope with incoming and unprocessed items: *stacking, spreading or stuffing*. Stackers usually feel pretty good about their method of organizing things. Typically each stack represents a different category of unprocessed items or separate, unfinished projects. Stacking things is certainly better than having no system and better than the second method...spreading. Spreaders do just that...they spread. They spread papers and things all about their offices. There is no real rhyme or reason behind the various spreading patterns in their workspace. Spreaders are usually quick to point out, *and some actually believe*, the following statement: "I know where everything is in these piles and stacks." This statement sounds good...but it is rarely true. And then there are the stuffers! Their offices look clean and neat, but if you look in their desks and file cabinets, you often find utter chaos. Papers and things are literally stuffed in their drawers.

So What?

If you are not reasonably organized, what message are you sending to others about your ability to handle your job responsibilities? If you are a stacker or spreader, the visible message may be that you are a bit disorganized...or you may be broadcasting that you are totally out of control. On the other hand, if you are a stuffer, you may appear to have your act together, but it is only a matter of time before your little secret is revealed and something falls through the cracks due to your underlying chaos. *It is important to understand that being organized is not just about being neat. Being organized means you can find things when you need them and that you consistently focus on important issues that support your true goals.* If you are able to operate at your best in a cluttered and chaotic environment, then you are a unique and fortunate person. However, if you struggle with workspace disorganization, or have concerns about the message your disorganization is sending your boss, co-workers or clients, you may need to rethink your workplace systems, processes and habits. Don't let one or more of the following reasons keep you from getting your workspace and workload in order:

- You think no one notices or cares about your disorganization.

- You stay so busy you do not feel you have the time to slow down and get things in order.

- You've tried getting organized before and could not find systems and processes that made it easy to get organized and stay organized.

Now What?

You think no one notices or cares. It has been my experience that it is very easy to buy into this idea if you have a long history of working in a messy and chaotic environment. Psychologists use the term habituation to describe the act of becoming accustomed to something, even extremely negative situations, through prolonged and frequent exposure. In other words, if you live with a mess long enough, you get used to it.

I've worked with a lot of people who simply do not care about their clutter and chaos...*until they are finally rid of it.* It is an absolute joy to see some of my clients let go of the illusion that it is easier to be disorganized than organized. That is what it has come to in our busy society...many people actually try to rationalize that life is easier when they are disorganized. Let's phrase that another way to make sure you get this important point: *Some people actually think that a disorganized life is better than an organized life.* I hope you aren't caught up in this illusion. Although many businesspeople are embracing this illusion now, the "mess is best" belief was previously more common among people in the artistic community. Artists feared that getting organized would rob them of their creativity and spontaneity. Many artists have now discovered that being reasonably organized and focused frees up huge blocks of time for their creative activities. Forget about the message you are sending to others for a moment and just focus on why you should care. You should care because your life will get better. You will get more done in less time and have more free time to do whatever it is that you want to do with your time.

As far as other people caring, take a chance if you think you can risk it, but don't be surprised if your chaos doesn't play so well with your boss and your clients. Look at the way you operate and the image your workspace projects through their eyes. Make sure you like what you see.

You stay too busy to slow down and get things in order. How many people do you know, or how many people have you heard about, who were finally slowed down or stopped in their tracks by an unexpected life event, *and came out on the other side of the tragedy in much better shape?* For example, the heart attack victim who finally realized how important it was to take care of his or her health, or the accident survivor who now cherishes the fact that he or she got a second chance to get things right with their family life. It shouldn't take a major, traumatic life event to convince you that busyness is rarely a sensible lifestyle choice. There is absolutely no guarantee that you will be around tomorrow. The best way to joyfully participate in life is to operate at a sensible, achievable, enjoyable life pace. You can skip the stress and drama of a life tragedy and enjoy all the benefits of a meaningful, joyful life by simply making a different choice when you wake up tomorrow. Choose to live a grounded, centered, well-paced life. Get your life in order and live every day as if it were the ultimate gift...it is!

You tried to get organized before and couldn't find an easy way to do it. I've realized in my career as an organizer that if I don't make what my clients are currently doing easier ...they will go back to their old habits. I don't blame them. Therefore, I specialize in ideas that meet three criteria:

1. They are easy to implement.

2. They cost little or nothing.

3. They take very little time each day.

Let me give you one example that will make life much easier for many of you. My clients often complain that they cannot get through all their reading material each day. Most of them are not speed-readers. I really don't propose that they become speed-readers. However, I do suggest that they learn to read faster. It's not really a big deal. For example, you can read a few pages (Pages 26-28 to be specific) of Bobbi DePorter and Mike Hernacki's book titled *Quantum Reading: The Power to Read Your Best*, and learn about a technique that will likely double your reading speed (and improve your comprehension and retention) with just a few minutes of practice. *The math is simple, if you double your reading speed, you cut your reading time in half, freeing up huge blocks of time to do other things.* Assuming you previously needed an hour a day to keep up with all your reading, this idea alone translates into over three weeks a year in freed up time.

By the way, this little speed-reading idea offers another significant benefit. You can easily get rid of the piles of unread material in your office. *What message are these piles, and the other piles of clutter in your office, sending to others about you? Is it the message you really want to send to everyone?*

Patti Schliep, CPO
Cascade Concierge
Kirkland, Washington

425.803.9577
yourassistant@earthlink.net
www.cascadeconcierge.com

Life is often too busy; even to the point of overwhelming. It's no wonder that many people desire to be more organized and productive in an effort to create a more balanced life.

Patti Schliep, owner of Cascade Concierge, has over 10 years of experience as an organizing consultant and personal assistant. She helps busy individuals accomplish more in less time and live more balanced lives. She also works with employees in businesses and corporations of all sizes to reduce stress, gain control, and more efficiently handle their workload.

Patti's background is as an educator and accounting profes-sional. She is a Certified Professional Organizer, a *Paper Tiger* Authorized Consultant (PTAC), a Certified *GO System* Trainer and a member of the National Association of Professional Organizers (NAPO). Her goal is to instruct, implement and guide individuals to a place of increased pro-ductivity, effectiveness and clarity.

22
The Paradox of Perfectionism
Patti Schliep

What?

How do you view perfectionism? Do you consider perfection-ism a badge of honor or an impossible standard that can never be attained? Being a perfectionist sounds like an admirable trait, especially when it's reinforced with observations from others such as: "She's an absolute wonder woman!" or "He does everything so well and can always be counted on to go the extra mile." But, the self-induced pressure of never being seen as less than perfect can be overwhelming or totally debil-itating to an uncompromising perfectionist.

It's normal for people to want to be good at what they do, but perfectionists have been defined by psychiatrist David D. Burns as people "whose standards are high beyond reach and reason" and "who strain compulsively and unremittingly toward impossible goals."

Instead of moving forward "perfectly" in life, work and inter-personal relationships, perfectionists constantly tread water or become hopelessly stalled in an effort to maintain a perceived image of infallibility. Even if you're not a perfectionist, it makes sense to understand how they view life since you often have to work with them to accomplish your own goals.

So What?

Although others appreciate their talents and skills, perfectionists often pay a high price for their ongoing quest to get things right...preferably the first time. Somewhere in their personal history, good just wasn't good enough and it became important for their projects to be "perfect."

Perfectionist tendencies often develop at an early age and are reinforced through subsequent life experiences. An individual may have thought (and been explicitly told) they weren't working hard enough to maintain the expectations and standards of a parent, teacher or coach. Appreciation and acceptance may have come only when they excelled or completed a task flawlessly. A general longing for acceptance, approval and external validation may have fueled an overpowering desire to perform at an unrealistic level.

Procrastination is often one of the first roadblocks encountered by perfectionists. Some perfectionists refuse to accept a task or tend to put off getting started on a task because they've set the bar too high. According to psychologist Joseph R. Ferrari, some procrastinators "would rather be seen as lacking in effort than lacking in ability." Unfortunately for the perfectionists/procrastinators, any initial relief gained from refusing to accept or putting off a project, eventually morphs into a highly stressful situation since perfectionists generally prefer not to be viewed as lacking in any way. Further aggravating their dilemma, a true perfectionist may not be capable of asking for assistance from others since that action in itself could be viewed as a personal weakness or failure.

The bottom line on perfectionism...a personal characteristic that appears on the surface to be a noble and desirable attribute shows its true colors. True perfectionism is a totally illogical, energy draining, potentially paralyzing pursuit. It keeps many highly talented, highly intelligent people from realizing their true potential in life.

Now What?

Mastering a skill or vocation is an enviable goal. However, the workplace and life do not revolve around everything being done "perfectly" the first time...or ever, for that matter. Here are a few ideas that may help you escape the burden of perfectionism.

Relax

Perfectionists are often told to relax, let go, lighten up a bit or not take themselves so seriously. If you have ever received similar advice while standing at a tee on the golf course, you may be able to relate to the inherent problem with such suggestions. The ability to simultaneously relax, swing easily, keep your eye on the ball, bend your knees, twist at the hips, keep your arm straight, and actually connect with the ball, all while aiming toward the green, using the proper club and not hitting a tree or sand trap is, shall we say, a bit difficult for someone who likes to get everything right the first time. This illustration gives you an ever so slight glimpse into the inner workings of the mind of a perfectionist...it just isn't that simple. Plenty of inner voices are already competing for the perfectionist's attention. Add a few external suggestions and you have a formula for paralyzing chaos.

Perfectionists must be able to give *themselves* permission to relax and refocus in order to calm their inner voices and create a productive mental environment. If you are a perfectionist...just focus on relaxing first. If you manage a perfectionist...relax and help them relax. Additional stress only perpetuates the productivity-killing cycle of perfectionism. Relax your breathing, relax your thinking and relax your standards. If you insist on being a perfectionist at something, become a perfectionist at relaxing.

Worry if You Must...Then Release Your Worries

Perfectionists tend to be worriers and may be viewed by others as caustic, combative or pessimistic, as they envision the potential problems that *may* arise as they work on a task. It's probably unrealistic to advise a perfectionist, or a recovering perfectionist, to stop worrying so much. If you must worry...go ahead...set aside a brief period of time each day to consider your worries. During that time, determine if your worries are rational, determine how much control you have over them, and decide on your options for dealing with them. Then, quickly do what you can do about them...and move on. If the worries reappear, make a commitment to get back to them during the next scheduled "worry period." Worrying is usually all about focusing on what you do not want to happen. Gradually learn to replace this kind of thinking with thoughts of what you do want to happen. Be patient with yourself. It takes time for the brain and nervous system to develop and adjust to new thought patterns.

A perfectionist's ability to envision obstacles and options can actually be a valuable skill. Relish the fact that you may be able to see the difficulties in completing a job that others might miss. Just don't let this skill get out of control and keep you from making forward progress.

As you encounter real or perceived obstacles, ask yourself, "Even if I don't succeed, what is the worst thing that might happen to me?" Is anything less than perfection failure or simply a signal to adjust, adapt or do things differently in the future? Isn't making mistakes a normal part of the learning process? Here's a novel idea (literally). If you want to seriously tackle the curse of perfectionism, read *When the Air Hits Your Brain: Tales of Neurosurgery* by Frank Vertosick, Jr., M.D. Learn what it takes to become a neurosurgeon and see if you think you could tolerate the nature and consequences of the mistakes they encounter on their learning journey. For most of you, it will put your day-to-day worries in a more proper perspective.

Rationally Use Time

Using your time pursuing excellence, mastery and other forms of personal activity that allow for growth as a human is rational. It is also human to make mistakes in the pursuit of such goals. If you *could* achieve perfectionism (assuming for a moment that there was such a thing), by definition your ability to experience further growth as a human would no longer exist. Come on...you know better...this is neither rational nor realistic. It is seriously flawed thinking. Ironically, pursuing perfectionism makes you an irrational (flawed) individual.

Reframe Your World

Columbus, Einstein and others reframed the way we look at and understand the world we live in. More recently, the Internet and other forms of technology have reframed the way we live and do business. Maybe it is time for you to reframe the way you look at mistakes. As children, we learn to walk by making mistakes; we learn to talk by making mistakes. Early in life, we basically learn almost everything by making mistakes and adjusting. Why should this natural learning process no longer be available to us as adults? Trying to minimize or avoid mistakes is a healthy life pursuit. Trying to eliminate the possibility of making a mistake is impossible and unproductive. Reframe your view of, and response to, mistakes in a way that will allow you to live an authentic and possible life, rather than an inauthentic and impossible life.

Oddly enough, when high-profile people who like to keep up the appearances of getting things right all the time, finally make a significant mistake that results in some sort of embarrassing public failure...they don't like it at first. However, soon after the initial embarrassment, some of them say they feel an overwhelming sense of relief. They may not like their circumstances, but the burden of living a perfect life is finally lifted. They can finally begin building an authentic life and no longer have to maintain the pretense of being a perfect person all the time.

Isn't it paradoxical that it often takes really big mistakes to finally cure perfectionists and help them get on a productive path in life?

J. Keith Sterne, CPA, CFP, CEBS
Financial Consulting Group, LLC
Germantown, Tennessee

901.309.2685
ksterne@fcgtn.com
www.fcgtn.com

Keith is managing partner and founder of Financial Consulting Group near Memphis, Tenn.

Graduating from the University of South Alabama with honors, he practiced as a CPA for nine years with KPMG. He worked for five years in investments and asset liability management for financial institutions serving with Union Planters National Bank as first vice president and Sendero Corporation as eastern regional manager. Keith has over 20 years of senior management experience consulting on retirement plans, incentives and executive compensation. As a part of his practice, he often consults with his clients on issues related to employee productivity, organization, career satisfaction and retention.

Keith has taught for the Bank Administration Institute (BAI) and Sam Houston Graduate Schools of Banking, and is the author of several articles on financial strategies, executive compensation and incentives.

23
The Value of Learning Groups
Keith Sterne

What?

"You'll be the same person in ten years as you are today except for the people you meet and the books you read."

– Charlie "Tremendous" Jones

"Charlie T" was commenting on the value of lifetime learning. He is a successful salesman, public speaker, author and teacher.

There are many similar quotes: *"Learn as if you were going to live forever."* – Gandhi; *"Wisdom is not a product of schooling, but of the lifelong attempt to acquire it."* – Einstein; *"I not only use all the brains that I have, but all that I can borrow."* – Woodrow Wilson; and on and on. That last one is particularly germane to this topic, since we are discussing learning in groups.

It is a sad thing when people think there is nothing new to learn. Look at kids. Children are like little learning locomotives. Everything is new to them and they have fun learning! We should all devote some time to being childlike and not so serious. Being too serious is like an illness; it is something to avoid. Maybe the drug companies will come out with an anti-seriousness pill!

Try to look at things differently, as if for the first time. Challenge some of your existing paradigms. It has been said that if you read one hour a day in your field that within three years you'll be an expert; in five, a top expert in the country; and in 10, in the world. Don't just confine learning to your work, however, pursue anything that interests you and that you enjoy. Remember to be childlike. Your life will be all the more rich and full as a result.

So What?

What can we do to learn more effectively and have fun doing it? How can we combine Charlie T's advice to read books *and* meet people? One way is to start a learning group.

For our purposes, a learning group is a collection of friends who agree to meet periodically to share ideas and experiences, help members solve problems and learn from one another.

Learning groups are used in higher education, church groups, businesses and informally. Called "collaborative learning" or "cooperative learning" in academia, it has been shown that students learn best when they are actively involved in the learning process. In one study, two groups of students were given material. One group was told they would be tested and graded on the material; the other was told they would have to teach it to the rest of the class. Guess which group learned more? The teaching group was more actively engaged with the material and achieved better mastery of the concepts. They were more successful in internalizing the ideas, since they had to prepare to teach them to others.

Being around bright, creative, motivated people is stimulating in and of itself. For most of us, it is usually more fun to work with the right group of people than to tackle a project alone.

Learning group participation also hones your presentation skills and allows you to gain more experience speaking before groups. Remember, most people say they fear public speaking more than a shark attack. Learning groups are a way to overcome some of these fears in front of a nonthreatening group of friends. If you can build solid presentation skills, they will be assets in almost any field of work.

Another advantage of being a part of a group is that you have "accountability partners" similar to Weight Watchers or Toastmasters. Knowing other like-minded people are involved helps you stay on track and get higher quality results. Don't make the learning group work, however. Remember the kids – have fun!

Now What?

So you think you want to start a group? How do you go about it; whom do you ask?

Start with friends you are comfortable with. I'm a member of a learning group that formed several years ago with a small group of friends. Keep things casual and low stress. We even share a bottle of wine occasionally during our group meetings. Something like that might work for you. Try to find people who are excited about learning: readers and "learning junkies" (enthusiast might be a better word). It's nice if the members feel it is something of a badge of honor to be invited into your group. True friends are supportive and help each other learn and grow.

The group is about learning; it is not intended to be a tool for business development. We don't exchange sales leads or expect members of the group to help market our products and services. That said, some business opportunities often naturally develop from participation in the group. It's not forbidden, it's just not the primary focus.

At a minimum, all members need to commit to attendance, participation and at least some leading/presenting. There will be members who are naturally more inclined to lead the group. Be careful not to let them take too much of the load or dominate the group.

How big should the group be? I would recommend starting out with a small group; say four or five friends/acquaintances. Larger groups decrease each member's opportunity to participate actively. Also, the less comfortable the group members are with presenting topics, the smaller the group should be. Once things get going and everyone is comfortable, you can add people. It is probably a good idea to have everyone's OK when inviting new members. Get people of diverse backgrounds; the learning experiences should be richer.

Almost any topic is fair game. It all depends on the members' interests and experience. In my group, we have had presentations about self-improvement, business, quantum physics, the workings of the brain and ancient Roman history. No matter the topic, it is good to try and relate the lessons to their use in everyday life.

Keep things low stress – remember the fun part! Allocate about an hour for the entire meeting – 30 minutes or so for the presentation, and the remainder for discussion. One person can be responsible for presenting a session or a topic can be divided between two or more people.

Think it's a good idea? Grab a partner and start recruiting! One more quote from the ubiquitous "Anonymous": *"Keep an open mind; your brain won't fall out!"*

Jan Wencel
Life Contained, Inc.
Naperville, Illinois

630.803.6650
jan@lifecontained.com
www.lifecontained.com

Most business professionals face information overload, the feeling of impermanence and increased expectations for output. These factors help create a desk piled high with papers, the constant pressure of deadlines, and a sense that there is no possibility of catching up. Jan's mission is to give hope and to impart new thinking to as many of these discouraged people as she can.

Jan is passionate about helping professionals live the life they always wanted: attentive to their responsibilities, balanced between work and play, and connected to the moment.

She began her career in the corporate world spending 12 years in advertising agencies. In 2002, Jan took a yearlong travel sabbatical (talk about being "de-velocitized"!). Then she pursued her lifelong passion for organizing by forming Life Contained.

She feeds her voracious appetite for new organizing methodologies through her *GO System* certification, and active memberships in the National Association of Professional Organizers (NAPO) and the Network for Productivity Excellence (NPEX).

24
Are You "Velocitized"?
Jan Wencel

What?

You've been driving 65 miles per hour on an interstate high-way for over two hours. For the last 100 miles or so, you've let the cruise control maintain your speed because you're more focused on singing along with your favorite music than driving. Nearing your destination, you exit onto a narrow country road...the music plays on. A mile or so after you exit, you look up and notice police lights flashing in your rearview mirror. You feel certain the police officer must be pursuing someone else. Ha...someone has broken the law and is about to get caught! He couldn't be after you...you haven't done anything wrong. As a matter of fact, you slowed considerably after exiting the interstate. Just to make sure, you glance at your speedometer. Uh oh...although it feels like you are driving at a snail's pace, you are stunned to discover you are going 45 miles per hour...in a 25 mile per hour zone! Unbelievable! You're driving at almost twice the speed limit. The policeman is stopping you! How could this be true?

The answer: You are velocitized.

Velocitization is a concept taught in many driver education classes. It occurs when you become acclimated to a certain rate of speed. When you're velocitized, you somehow experience the sensation of moving much slower than your actual speed.

If you're like most Americans, you approach your work and much of your leisure time in a velocitized state. You grow accustomed to the fast pace and never slow down to a more reasonable, enjoyable and productive life pace.

So What?

In our fast-paced society, most of us feel compelled to be productive 24/7. In some circles, this compulsion has grown to lunacy. People consider after-midnight e-mails badges of honor and proof of their stamina and diligence. Those who work 70+ hour weeks flaunt their time sheets like status symbols. In our upside-down world of too much work and too little play, we often confuse speed and busyness with being productive.

The February 2002 *Harvard Business Review* article, "Beware the Busy Manager," reported that a mere 10 percent of the managers surveyed spent their time in a committed, purposeful and reflective manner (another 40 percent of these supposedly cream-of-the-crop managers confused frantic motion/busyness with constructive action, 30 percent were master procrastinators, and 20 percent were totally disengaged). The article went on to describe characteristics differentiating successful managers from the unsuccessful. Based on this survey and my personal experience with high-performing managers, successful managers share at least two important qualities:

- They are adept at conserving their energy and using it wisely. For example, some only respond to e-mails, phone calls or visitors at certain times of the day (usually after they have spent an appropriate amount of time focusing on their priorities for the day). Others proactively build "think time" into their schedules.

- They are skilled at finding ways to take care of both sides of the human energy equation. They schedule time to physically and emotionally re-energize *and* they develop strategies to reduce energy-draining stress. They frequently participate in activities that allow them to tap into their personal source of positive energy. Some work out at the gym or get involved in sports. Others share their fears, frustrations and thoughts about work with a partner, friend or colleague. Still others refuel their inner reserves through hobbies like gardening or fishing.

What can this teach us? When we learn to slow down and insert thoughtful, energy-replenishing leisure time into our lives, speed and quantity are replaced by a more enjoyable, productive life pace, and quality. In other words, we become the illusive "person living a balanced life" that we hear so much about, but rarely encounter.

Now What?

So how do you forgo your tendency for speed and quantity, and recalibrate efforts to achieve balance and quality? How do you keep your energy source replenished? Here are a few ideas to consider if you desire to live more joyfully and productively.

Slow down to 25 miles per hour and savor leisure time. If you're anything like me, you are inclined to move at high speeds when you are engaged in leisure activities. It's bad enough to do this at work, but leisure time should help prevent burnout...not accelerate it. Try symbolically "looking in the rearview mirror" when you are engaged in leisure activities. If you sense the equivalent of flashing lights, check your speed. Slow down and take it easy.

Truly free up your free time. Leisure time is not about efficiency and effectiveness. Leisure time is about disengaging from your normal routine, relaxing and replenishing your energy. For instance, don't handle work calls while taking a walk. Instead, engage in the process of walking at a comfortable pace and connect with your surroundings. Consider not going online while watching television. Alternately, if you are watching TV, try to relate to the program with your full self. Laugh from the belly at the funny parts. Sob from the heart at the sad scenes. During your free time, focus on activities (or periods of inactivity) that restore your energy and nurture your body and soul.

Do not allow work to interrupt your time off. Ignore business calls and e-mails as much as possible on your days off and when you are on vacation. For example, free yourself from the habit of checking work e-mail from home every night, and avoid business calls at family functions. Leave your handheld device at home on your bike ride. If you go online to find movie listings, resist the temptation to research something for work. You get the idea.

Find out what gives you energy and repeat it as often as necessary. If you don't already know what gives your life energy, spend some time finding out. Is it biking, entertaining friends, golfing, yoga or discussing politics? The choices are limitless, but you need to identify what works best for you in order to consistently renew your energy. Next, schedule these activities on your calendar with regularity. If you find you're getting easily frustrated at work or at home, rank your personal well-being level on a scale of 1 to 10, with 10 being "couldn't feel much better." If your ranking is low, then it's time to slow down and make some changes in your daily routine.

Add think time to your schedule. Not every moment at work needs to be consumed with frantic motion. Purposely add contemplation time to your daily schedule. Some of your best work and best ideas will grow out of your periods of stillness and reflection.

Develop a reputation for being deliberate, but not fast. For instance, if you fire back e-mail responses within nanoseconds of their arrival, you are setting the expectation that you constantly monitor your e-mail. Try turning off your e-mail notifications. Read and answer e-mail two or three times a day, and stay focused on your priorities and the tasks at hand. This allows you to deliver quality responses on your own time, and allows you to operate at an even pace throughout the day. It also teaches your colleagues to expect deliberate, but not instantaneous, responses.

Enlist a police officer. Until you develop a more appropriate work and life pace, you might consider asking someone to police you and to keep you honest. Enlist the help of a co-worker, a superior, a close friend or your spouse. Just make certain it's someone you respect, someone who has your best interest in mind, and someone who will hold you accountable.

Although we have no road signs to tell us how fast to work or how slow to play, we must occasionally employ techniques to "de-velocitize" our lives and work toward operating at a productive, fulfilling and life-nurturing pace. Our goal shouldn't just be getting the most out of life...our true goal should be to get the *best* out of life.